MEDIEVAL INDIA

FROM
CONTEMPORARY SOURCES

EXTRACTS FROM ARABIC AND PERSIAN ANNALS
AND EUROPEAN TRAVELS

MEDIEVAL INDIA

FROM
CONTEMPORARY SOURCES

EXTRACTS FROM ARABIC AND PERSIAN ANNALS
AND EUROPEAN TRAVELS

EDITED BY

STANLEY LANE-POOLE,

M.A. (Oxon.), Litt. D.

SOMETIME PROFESSOR OF ARABIC AND PERSIAN
IN THE UNIVERSITY OF DUBLIN

GYAN

Published by

GYAN

Gyan Publishing House
5, Ansari Road
Daryaganj, New Delhi-110002
Phone: 011-47034999, 9811692060
E-mail: books@gyanbooks.com

Distribution Network
gyanbooks.com
India, USA, Canada, UK, Australia, France

ISBN : 978-81-212-2786-5 (HB)
First Published, 1917

2nd Impression 2021

Printed at: Gyan Press, Delhi.

Medieval India
Edited by: Stanley Lane-Poole

MEDIEVAL INDIA

FROM

CONTEMPORARY SOURCES

EXTRACTS FROM ARABIC AND PERSIAN ANNALS
AND EUROPEAN TRAVELS

EDITED BY

STANLEY LANE-POOLE, M.A. (Oxon.), Litt. D.

SOMETIME PROFESSOR OF ARABIC AND PERSIAN
IN THE UNIVERSITY OF DUBLIN

BOMBAY

K. & J. COOPER

EDUCATIONAL PUBLISHERS

PREFACE

These extracts are intended to show how contemporary chroniclers and (in the later period) European travellers described some of the chief events and rulers of medieval India, from the incursions of Mahmud of Ghazni about 1000 to 1764 when, after the shattering of the Maratha domination, the English took the Great Mogul under their protection and laid the foundations of the present Empire in India. The diffuse and elaborate style of the Persian writers, most of whom were bigoted Muslims, has been in many cases freely pruned or paraphrased, since no advantage would be gained in a book of this kind by a literal reproduction of Elliott and Dowson's translations, from which most of the earlier extracts are derived; but the records of European travellers and the more recent and very accurate translations of living scholars have merely been abridged, though the spelling of oriental names has been made to confirm to that adopted throughout the book. Editorial insertions are placed within square brackets. The extracts are arranged in approximately chronological order. The names of the authors and the works cited are given at the head of each extract. As no proofs can be sent to me for correction, I must apologize in advance for any slips.

For permission to print extracts from their translations I wish to express my cordial thanks to Mrs. Beveridge (for Gul-badan's Memoirs; and Babur's Memoirs, the latter translated from the original Turki, by which I have emended Erskine and Leyden's version), Mr. Beveridge (for the Akbarnama and Jahangir's Memoirs), Colonel H. S. Jarrett (for the Aïn-i-Akbari), Dr. E. Denison Ross (for the Ta'rikh-i-Rashidi), and to the Council of the Royal Asiatic Society for leave to print extracts from the Society's publication of the Memoirs of Jahangir, translated by A. Rogers and H. Beveridge.

STANLEY LANE-POOLE

CONTENTS.

MEDIEVAL INDIA

FROM CONTEMPORARY SOURCES.

—1—

DEFEAT OF JAIPAL.

[Al-'Utbi: *Ta'rikh Yamini.*]

Sultan Mahmud at first designed in his heart to go to Sijistan, but subsequently preferred engaging previously in a holy
1001. war against Hind, and he distributed arms prior to convening a council on the subject, in order to secure a blessing on his designs of exalting the standard of religion, of widening the plain of right, of illuminating the words of truth, and of strengthening the power of justice. He departed towards the country of Hind in full reliance on the aid of God, who guiding by his light and by his power bestowed dignity upon him and gave him victory in all his expeditions. On his reaching Peshawar, he pitched his tent outside the city. There he received intelligence of the bold resolve of Jaipal, the enemy of God, and King of Hind, to offer opposition, and of his rapid advance towards meeting his fate in the field of battle. He then took a muster of his horses and of all his warriors and their vassals from those in whose records it was entered, and then selected from among his troops 15,000 cavalry, men and officers, all bold, and strictly prohibited those who were rejected and not fit or disposed for war from joining those who had been chosen and who were like dragons of the desert and lions of the forest.

With them he advanced against the wicked and accursed enemy, whose hearts were firm as hills and were as twigs of patience on boughs of affection. The villainous infidel came forward, proud in his numbers and strength of head and arm, with 12,000 horsemen, 30,000 foot soldiers, and 300 elephants, at the ponderous weight of which the lighter earth groaned; little reflecting that, under God's dispensation, a small army can overturn a host; as the ignorant man would have learnt, could he have read the word of God:—"Oftentimes a small army overcomes a large one by the order of God."

That infidel remained where he was, avoiding the action for a long time, and awaiting craftily the arrival of reinforcements and other vagabond families and tribes which were on their way; but the Sultan would not allow him to postpone the conflict, and the friends of God commenced the action, setting upon the enemy with sword, arrow, and spear, plundering, seizing, and destroying; at all which the Hindus, being greatly alarmed, began to kindle the flame of fight. The Hindu set his cavalry in order and beat his drums. The elephants moved on from their posts, and line advanced against line, shooting their arrows at one another like boys escaped from school, who at eventime shoot at a target for a wager. Swords flashed like lightning amid the blackness of clouds, and fountains of blood flowed like the fall of setting stars. The friends of God defeated their obstinate opponents and quickly put them to a complete rout. Noon had not arrived when the Muslims had wreaked their vengeance on the infidel enemies of God, killing 15,000 of them, spreading them like a carpet over the ground, and making them food for beasts and birds of prey. Fifteen elephants fell on the field of battle, as their legs, being pierced with arrows, became as motionless as if they had been in a quagmire, and their trunks were cut with the swords of the valiant heroes.

The enemy of God, Jaipal, and his children and grand-children and nephews and the chief men of his tribe and his relations, were taken prisoners, and being strongly bound with ropes were carried before the Sultan like as evildoers on whose faces the fumes of infidelity are evident, who are covered with the vapours of misfortune, will be bound and carried to hell. Some had their arms forcibly tied behind their backs, some were seized by the cheek, some were driven by blows on the neck. The necklace was taken off the neck of Jaipal, composed of large pearls and shining gems and rubies set in gold, of which the value was two hundred thousand dinars; and twice that value was obtained from the necks of those of his relations who were taken prisoners or slain, and had become the food of the mouths of hyenas and vultures. God also bestowed upon his friends such an amount of booty as was beyond all bounds and all calculation, including five hundred thousand slaves, beautiful men and women. The Sultan returned with his followers to his camp, having plundered immensely, by God's aid, having obtained the victory, and thankful to God, the lord of the universe. For the Almighty had given them victory over a province of the country of Hind, broader and longer and more fertile than Khurasan. This splendid and celebrated action took place on Thursday, the 8th of Muharram, 392 H. [27th November 1001].

—2—

INVASION OF HINDUSTAN.

[Firishta.]

In the year 399 H. Mahmud, having collected his forces, determined again to invade Hindustan, and punish Anandpal,

the son of Jaipal, who had shown much insolence during his late invasion of Multan. Anandpal hearing of his in-
1008. tentions, sent ambassadors on all sides inviting the assistance of the other princes of Hindustan, who now considered the expulsion of the Muhammadans from India as a sacred duty. Accordingly, the Rajas of Ujjain, Gwalior, Kalinjar, Kanauj, Delhi, and Ajmir, entered into a confederacy, and collecting their forces advanced towards the Panjab with a greater army than had ever taken the field against Amir Sabuktigin. Anandpal himself took the command and advanced to meet the invader. The Indians and Muhammadans arrived in sight of each other on the plain of Peshawar, where they remained encamped forty days, neither side shewing any eagerness to come to action. The troops of the idolaters daily increased in number and aid came to them from all sides. The infidel Khokhars also joined them in great strength, and made extraordinary exertions to resist the Muslims. The Hindu females on this occasion sold their jewels and sent the proceeds from distant parts to their husbands, so that they being supplied with all necessaries for the march might be in earnest in the war. Those who were poor contributed from their earnings by spinning cotton and other labour. The Sultan perceived that on this occasion the idolaters behaved most devotedly and that it was necessary to be very circumspect in striking the first blow. He therefore entrenched his camp, that the infidels might not be able to penetrate therein.

Mahmud, having thus secured himself, ordered six thousand archers to the front to attack and endeavour to draw the enemy near to his entrenchments, where the Muslims were prepared to receive them. In spite of the Sultan's precautions, during the heat of the battle 30,000 infidel Khokhars, with their heads and feet bare, and armed with spears and other weapons, penetrated on two sides into the Muhammadan lines, and forcing their way into the midst of the cavalry, they cut down men and horse with their swords, daggers, and spears, so that, in a few minutes, they slaughtered three or four thousand Muslims. They carried their success so far that the Sultan, observing the fury of these Khokhar footmen, withdrew himself from the thick of the fight that he might stop the battle for that day. But it so happened that the elephant upon which Anandpal rode, becoming unruly from the effects of naphtha balls and the flights of arrows, turned and fled. The Hindus, deeming this to be the signal for flight on the part of their general, all gave way and fled, so that 8,000 Hindus were killed in the retreat. Thirty elephants and enormous booty fell into the hands of the pursuers, with which they returned to the Sultan.

—3—

SACKING OF SOMNAT.

[Ibn-al-Athir: *Kamil.*]

In the year 414 H. Mahmud captured several forts and cities in Hind, and he also took the idol called Somnat. This
1024. idol was the greatest of any of the idols of Hind. Every night that there was an eclipse, the Hindus went on a pilgrimage to the temple and there congregated to the number of a hundred thousand persons. They believed that the souls of men after separation from the body used to meet there, according to their doctrine of transmigration, and that the ebb and flow of the tide was the worship paid to the idol by the sea to the best of its power. Everything of the

most precious was brought there; its attendants received the most valuable presents, and the temple was endowed with more than 10,000 villages. In the temple were amassed jewels of the most exquisite quality and incalculable value. The people of India have a great river called Gang, to which they pay the highest honour and into which they cast the bones of their great men in the belief that the deceased will thus secure an entrance to heaven. Between this river and Somnat there is a distance of about 200 parasangs, but water was daily brought from it with which the idol was washed. One thousand Brahmans attended every day to perform the worship of the idol and to introduce the visitors. Three hundred persons were employed in shaving the heads and beards of the pilgrims. Three hundred and fifty persons sang and danced at the gate of the temple. Everyone of these received a settled allowance daily. When Mahmud was gaining victories and demolishing idols in India, the Hindus said that Somnat was displeased with these idols and that if he had been satisfied with them no one could have destroyed or injured them.

When Mahmud heard this he resolved upon making a campaign to destroy this idol, believing that, when the Hindus saw their prayers and imprecations to be false and futile, they would embrace the faith. So he prayed to the Almighty for aid, and left Ghazni on the 10th Sha'ban, 414 H. with 30,000 horse besides volunteers, and took the road to Multan, which place he reached in the middle of Ramazan. The road from thence to India was through a barren desert, where there were neither inhabitants nor food. So he collected provisions for the passage and loading 30,000 camels with water and corn he started for Anhalwara. After he had crossed the desert, he perceived on one side a fort full of people, in which place there were wells. People came down to conciliate him, but he invested the place, and God gave him victory over it; for the hearts of the inhabitants failed them through fear. So he brought the place under the sway of Islam, killed the inhabitants, and broke in pieces their images. His men carried water away with them from thence and marched for Anhalwara, where they arrived at the beginning of Zu-l-ka'da.

The chief of Anhalwara, called Bhim, fled hastily and abandoning his city went to a certain fort for safety and to prepare himself for war. Mahmud again started for Somnat, and on his march he came to several forts in which were many images serving as chamberlains or heralds of Somnat, and accordingly he called them Shaitan. He killed the people who were in these places, destroyed the fortifications, broke in pieces the idols, and continued his march to Somnat through a desert where there was little water. There he met 20,000 fighting men, inhabitants of that country, whose chiefs would not submit. So he sent some forces against them, who defeated them, put them to flight, and plundered their possessions. From thence they marched to Dabalwarah, which is two days' journey from Somnat. The people of this place stayed resolutely in it, believing that Somnat would utter his prohibition and drive back the invaders; but Mahmud took the place, slew the men, plundered their property, and marched on to Somnat.

He reached Somnat on a Thursday in the middle of Zu-l-ka'da, and there he beheld a strong fortress built upon the sea shore, so that it was washed by the waves. The people of the fort were on the walls amusing themselves at the expense of the confident Muslims, telling them that their deity would cut off the last man of them and destroy them all. On the morrow, which was Friday, the assailants advanced to the assault, and when the Hindus beheld the Muhammadans fighting, they abandoned their posts and left the walls. The Muslims planted their ladders against the walls and gained the summit; then they proclaimed their success with their religious war-cry and exhibited the prowess of Islam. Then followed a fearful slaughter and matters wore a serious aspect. A body of Hindus hurried to Somnat, cast themselves on the ground before him, and besought him to grant them victory. Night came on and the fight was suspended.

Next morning early the Muhammadans renewed the battle and made greater havoc among the Hindus, till they drove them from the town to the house of their idol Somnat. A dreadful slaughter followed at the gate of the temple. Band after band of defenders entered the temple to Somnat and with their hands clasped round their necks wept and passionately entreated him. Then again they issued forth to fight until they were slain, and but few were left alive. Those took to the sea in boats to make their escape, but the Muslims overtook them, and some were killed and some were drowned.

This temple of Somnat was built upon fifty-six pillars of teak wood covered with lead. The idol itself was in a chamber; its height was five cubits and its girth three cubits. This was what appeared to the eye, but two cubits were [hidden] in the basement. It had no appearance of having been sculptured. Mahmud seized it, part of it he burnt, and part of it he carried away with him to Ghazni, where he made it a step at the entrance of the Jami' mosque. The shrine of the idol was dark, but it was lighted by most exquisitely jewelled chandeliers. Near the idol was a chain of gold to which bells were attached. The weight of it was 200 maunds [*man*]. When a certain portion of the night had passed, this chain was shaken to ring the bells and so rouse a fresh party of Brahmans to carry on the worship. The treasury was near and in it there were many idols of gold and silver. Over it there were veils hanging, set with jewels, every one of which was of immense value. The worth of what was found in the temple exceeded two millions of dinars, all of which was taken. The number of the slain exceeded fifty thousand.

—4—

AMIR MAS'UD HAS A DRINKING PARTY.

[Baihaki : *Ta'rikh Sabuktigin.*]

On Tuesday the 12th of Muharram the Amir went to the Firozi Garden [at Ghazni] and sat in the Green Pavilion on
1040. the Golden Plain. A sumptuous feast was ordered and messes of pottage were set round. The Amir Maudud and the Minister came and sat down, and the army passed in review before them. First passed the star of Amir Maudud, the canopy, waving standards, and two hundred slaves of the household with jackets of mail and spears, and many led horses and camels, and infantry with their banners displayed, and a hundred and seventy slaves fully armed and equipped with all their stars borne before them. After them came Irtigin the Chamberlain and his slaves to the number of eighty, and then fifty military slaves of the household, preceded by twenty officers finely accoutred, with many led horses and camels, followed by other officers till all had passed.

It was now near mid-day prayer, when the Amir bade his son and the minister and the chief chamberlain and the officers to sit down to the feast. He too sat down and ate bread, and then they all took their leave and departed. "It was the last time they looked on that king [God's mercy on him !]."

After their departure the Amir said to 'Abd-ar-Razzak, "What say you, shall we drink a little wine?" He replied, "When can we better drink than on such a day as this, when my lord is happy, and my lord's son has attained his wish and departed with the minister and officers:—especially after eating such a dinner as this?" The Amir said, "Let us begin without ceremony, for we have come into the country, and we will drink in the Firozi Garden." Accordingly much wine was brought immediately from the pavilion into the garden, and fifty goblets and flagons were placed in the middle of a small tent. The goblets were sent round and the Amir said, "Let us keep fair measure and fill the cups evenly, in order that there may be no unfairness." Each goblet contained nearly a pint. They began to get jolly and the minstrels sang. Bu-l-Hasan drank five goblets, his head was affected at the sixth, he lost his senses at the seventh, and began to vomit at the eighth, when the servants carried him off. Bu-l-'Ala the physician dropped his head at the fifth cup, and he also was carried off. Khalil Da'ud drank ten; Siyabiruz nine; and both were borne away to the hill of Dailaman. Bu-Na'im drank twelve and ran off. Da'ud Maimandi fell down drunk, and the singers and buffoons all rolled off tipsy, when the Sultan and Khwaja 'Abd-ar-Razzak alone remained. When the Khwaja had drunk eighteen cups, he made his obeisance and prepared to go, saying to the Amir, "If you give your slave any more, he will lose his respect for your Majesty as well as his own wits." The Amir laughed and gave him leave to go; when he got up and departed in a most respectful manner. After this the Amir kept on drinking and enjoying himself. He drank twenty-seven full goblets of half a maund each. He then arose, called for a basin of water and his praying carpet, washed his face, and read the mid-day prayers as well as the afternoon ones, and so acquitted himself that you would have said he had not drunk a single cup. He then got on an elephant and returned to the Palace. I witnessed the whole of this scene with mine own eyes — I, Abu-l-Fazl.

— 5 —

BATTLES OF TARAÏN.

[Minhaj-i-Siraj : *Tabakat-i-Nasiri.*]

Raï Kolah Pithaura [or Prithvi] came up against the fort, and the Sultan [Muhammad Ghori] returned and faced him at Taraïn. All the Raïs of Hindustan were with

1191-2. the Raï Kolah. The battle was formed and the Sultan, seizing a lance, made a rush upon the elephant which carried Gobind Raï of Delhi. The latter advanced to meet him in front of the battle, and then the Sultan, who was a second Rustam and the Lion of the Age, drove his lance into the mouth of the Raï and knocked two of the accursed wretch's teeth down his throat. The Raï, on the other hand, returned the blow and inflicted a severe wound on the arm of his adversary. The Sultan reined back his horse and turned aside, and the pain of the wound was so insufferable that he could not support himself on horseback. The Muslim army gave way and could not be controlled. The Sultan was just falling, when a sharp and brave young Khalji recognized him, jumped upon the horse behind him, and clasping him round the bosom spurred on the horse and bore him from the midst of the fight.

When the Muslims lost sight of the Sultan, a panic fell upon them; they fled and halted not until they were safe from the pursuit of the victors. A party of nobles and youths of Ghor had seen and recognized their leader with that lion-hearted

Khalji, and when he came up they drew together, and, forming a kind of litter with broken lances, they bore him to the bathing-place. The hearts of the troops were consoled by his appearance, and the Muhammadan faith gathered new strength in his life. He collected the scattered forces and retreated to the territories of Islam, leaving Kazi Tolak in the fort of Sirhind. Raï Pithaura advanced and invested the fort, which he besieged for thirteen months.

Next year the Sultan assembled another army, and advanced into Hindustan to avenge his defeat. A trustworthy person, one of the principal men of the hills of Tolak, informed me that he was in this army, and that its force amounted to one hundred and twenty thousand horsemen bearing armour. Before the Sultan could arrive the fort of Sirhind had capitulated, and the enemy were encamped in the vicinity of Taraïn. The Sultan drew up his battle array, leaving his main body in the rear, with the banners, canopies, and elephants, to the number of several divisions. His plan of attack being formed, he advanced quietly. The light unarmoured horsemen were made into four divisions of 10,000 and were directed to advance and harass the enemy on all sides, on the right and on the left, in the front and in the rear, with their arrows. When the enemy collected his forces to attack, they were to support each other and to charge at full speed. By these tactics the infidels were worsted; the Almighty gave us the victory over them, and they fled.

Pithaura alighted from his elephant, mounted a horse and galloped off, but he was captured near Sarsuti and sent to hell. Gobind Raï, of Delhi was killed in the battle, and the Sultan recognized his head by the two teeth which he had broken. The capital, Ajmir, and all the Siwalik hills, Hansi, Sarsuti, and other districts were the results of this victory, which was gained in the year 588 H. [1192].

—6—

CAPTURE OF BENARES.

[Ibn-al-Athir: *Kamil.*]

Shihab-ad-din [Muhammad] Ghori, king of Ghazni, sent his slave Kutb-ad-din [Aibak] to make war against the provinces of Hind, and this general made an incursion in
1194. which he killed many and returned home with prisoners and booty. The king of Benares was the greatest king in India and possessed the largest territory, extending lengthwise from the borders of China to the province of Malwa and in breadth from the sea to within ten days' journey of Lahore. When he was informed of this inroad, he collected his forces, and in the year 590 H. [1194], he entered the territories of the Muhammadans. Shihab-ad-din Ghori marched forth to oppose him, and the two armies met on the river Jumna, which is a river about as large as the Tigris at Mosul. The Hindu prince had seven hundred elephants and his men were said to amount to a million. There were many nobles in his army. There were Muslims in that country since the days of Mahmud ibn Sabuktigin who continued faithful to the law of Islam and constant in prayer and good works. When the two armies met, there was great carnage; the infidels were sustained by their numbers and the Muslims by their courage; but in the end the infidels fled and the faithful were victorious. The slaughter of Hindus was immense; none was spared, except women and children, and the carnage of the men went on until the earth was weary. Ninety elephants were captured, and of the rest some were killed, and some escaped. The Hindu king was slain, and no one would have recognized his corpse

but for the fact of his teeth, which were weak at their roots, being fastened in with golden wire. After the flight of the Hindus, Shihab-ad-din entered Benares and carried off its treasures upon fourteen hundred camels. He then returned to Ghazni. Among the elephants which were captured there was a white one. A person who saw it told me that when the elephants were brought before Shihab-ad-din and were ordered to salute, they all saluted except the white one.

— 7 —

CONQUEST OF NUDIYA.

[Minhaj-i-Siraj: *Tabakat-i-Nasiri.*]

Let us return to the history of Muhammad ibn Bakhtyar. When he came back from his visit to Sultan Kutb-ad-din and
1199. conquered Bihar, his fame reached the ears of Raï Lakhmaniya and spread throughout all parts of the Raï's dominions. A body of astrologers, Brahmans and wise men of the kingdom, came to the Raï and represented to him that in their books the old Brahmans had written that the country would eventually fall into the hands of the Turks. The time appointed was approaching; the Turks had already taken Bihar, and next year they would also attack his country; it was therefore advisable that the Raï should make peace with them, so that all the people might emigrate from the territory and save themselves from contention with the Turks. The Raï asked whether the man who was to conquer the country was described as having any peculiarity in his person. They replied, Yes: the peculiarity is, that in standing upright both his hands hang down below the knees, so that his fingers

touch his shins. The Raï observed that it was best for him to send some confidential agents to make enquiry about that peculiarity. Accordingly confidential agents were despatched, an examination was made, and the peculiarity was found in the person of Muhammad ibn Bakhtyar. When this was ascertained to be the fact, most of the Brahmans and many chiefs went away, but Raï Lakhmaniya did not like to leave his territory.

Next year Muhammad ibn Bakhtyar prepared an army and marched from Bihar. He suddenly appeared before the city of Nudiya with only eighteen horsemen; the remainder of his army was left to follow. Muhammad ibn Bakhtyar did not molest any man but went on peaceably and without ostentation, so that no one could suspect who he was. The people rather thought that he was a merchant who had brought horses for sale. In this manner he reached the gate of Raï Lakhmaniya's palace, when he drew his sword and commenced the attack. At this time the Raï was at his dinner, and golden and silver dishes filled with food were placed before him according to the usual custom. All of a sudden a cry was raised at the gate of his palace and in the city.

Before he had ascertained what had occurred, Muhammad ibn Bakhtyar had rushed into the palace and put a number of men to the sword. The Raï fled barefooted by the rear of the palace, and his whole treasure and all his wives, maid-servants, attendants, and women fell into the hands of the invader. Numerous elephants were taken and such booty was obtained by the Muhammadans as is beyond all compute. When his army arrived the whole city was brought under subjection and he fixed his headquarters there.

—8—

SULTAN RAZIYA, DAUGHTER OF ALTAMISH.

[Minhaj-i-Siraj: *Tabakat-i-Nasiri.*]

Sultan Raziya was a great monarch. She was wise, just and generous, a benefactor to her kingdom, a dispenser of justice, the protector of her subjects, and the leader of
1236-40. her armies. She was endowed with all the qualities befitting a king; but she was not born of the right sex, and so in the estimation of men all these virtues were worthless. [May God have mercy on her!] In the time of her father she had exercised authority with great dignity. Her mother was the chief wife of his Majesty, and she resided in the chief royal palace in Kushk-i-firozi. The Sultan discerned in her countenance the signs of power and bravery, and although she was a girl and lived in retirement, yet when the Sultan returned from the conquest of Gwalior, he directed his secretary who was director of the government, to put her name in writing as heir of the kingdom and successor to the throne. Before this farman was executed, the servants of the State, who were in close intimacy with his Majesty, represented that, seeing the king had grown-up sons who were worthy of the dignity, what wisdom could there be in making a woman the heir to a Muhammadan throne and what advantage could accrue from it? They besought him to set their minds at ease, for the course that he proposed seemed very inexpedient. The King replied, "My sons are devoted to the pleasures of youth, and no one of them is qualified to be king. They are unfit to rule the country, and after my death you will find that there is no one more competent to guide the State than my daughter." It was afterwards agreed by common consent that the King had judged wisely.

—9—

KING BALBAN.

[Barani: *Ta'rikh-i-Firoz-Shahi.*]

In the first year after his accession, the ripe judgement and experience of Balban was directed in the first place to the organization of his army, for the army is the source
1266. and means of government. The cavalry and infantry, both old and new, were placed under the command of *maliks* of experience, of chiefs who held the first rank in their profession, and were brave, dignified and faithful. In the first and second year he assumed great state, and made great display of his pomp and dignity. Muslims and Hindus would come from distances of one or two hundred leagues [*kos* = $2\frac{1}{2}$ miles] to see the splendour of his equipage, which filled them with amazement. No sovereign had ever before exhibited such pomp and grandeur in Delhi. For the twenty-two years that Balban reigned he maintained the dignity, honour, and majesty of the throne in a manner that could not be surpassed. Certain of his attendants who waited on him in private assured me that they never saw him otherwise than full-dressed. During the whole time that he was Khan and Sultan, extending over nearly forty years, he never conversed with persons of low origin or occupation, and never indulged in any familiarity, either with friends or strangers, by which the dignity of the Sovereign could be lowered. He never joked with any one, nor did he allow any one to joke in his presence; he never laughed aloud, nor did he permit any one in his Court to laugh. As long as he lived no officer or acquaintance dared to recommend for employment any

person of low position or extraction. In the administration of justice he was inflexible, showing no favour to his brethren or children, to his associates or attendants; and if any of them committed an act of injustice, he never failed to give redress and comfort to the injured person. No man dared to be too severe to his slaves or handmaids, to his horsemen or footmen.

—10—

'ALA-AD-DIN KHALJI.

[Barani: *Ta'rikh-i-Firoz-Shahi.*]

In the third year of his reign 'Ala-ad-din had little to do beyond attending to his pleasures, giving feasts, and holding festivals. One success followed another; des-
1299. patches of victory came in from all sides; every year he had two or three sons born; affairs of State went on according to his wish and to his satisfaction, his treasury was overflowing, boxes and caskets of jewels and pearls were daily displayed before his eyes, he had numerous elephants in his stables and seventy thousand horses in the city and environs; two or three regions were subject to his sway, and he had no apprehension of enemies to his kingdom or of any rival to his throne. All this prosperity intoxicated him. Vast desires and great aims, far beyond him or a hundred thousand like him, formed their germs in his brain, and he entertained fancies which had never occurred to any king before him. In his exaltation, ignorance, and folly he quite lost his head, forming the most impossible schemes and nourishing the most extravagant desires. He was a man of no learning and never associated with men of learning. He could not read or

write a letter. He was bad-tempered, obstinate, and hard-hearted; but the world smiled upon him, fortune befriended him, and his schemes were generally successful, so he only became the more reckless and arrogant.

—11—

POLICY OF 'ALA-AD-DIN.

[Barani: *Ta'rikh-i-Firoz-Shahi.*]

The Sultan next turned his attention to preventing rebellion, and first by confiscation of property. Whenever a village was held by proprietary right, in free gift, or as a religious endowment, it was to be brought back into the exchequer by a stroke of the pen. The people were pressed and amerced and money was exacted from them on every kind of pretext. All pensions, grants of land, and endowments were appropriated. The people became so absorbed in trying to keep themselves alive that rebellion was never mentioned. Next, he set up so minute a system of espionage that nothing done, good or bad, was hidden from him. No one could stir without his knowledge, and whatever happened in the houses of nobles, grandees, and officials was brought by his spies for his information, and their reports were acted on. To such a length did this prying go that nobles dared not speak aloud even in thousand-columned palaces, but had to communicate by signs. In their own houses, night and day, dread of the spies made them tremble. What went on in the bazars was all reported and controlled.

Thirdly, he forbade wine, beer, and intoxicating drugs to be used or sold; dicing, too, was prohibited. Vintners and beer sellers were turned out of the city, and the heavy taxes which had been levied from them were abolished. All the china and glass vessels of the Sultan's banquetting room were broken and thrown outside the gate of Badaun, where they formed a mound. Jars and casks of wine were emptied out there till they made mire as if it were the season of the rains. The Sultan himself entirely gave up wine parties. Self-respecting people at once followed his example; but the ne'er-do-wells went on making wine and spirits and hid the leather bottles in loads of hay or firewood and by various such tricks smuggled it into the city. Inspectors and gatekeepers and spies diligently sought to seize the contraband and the smugglers; and when seized the wine was given to the elephants, and the importers and sellers and drinkers flogged and given short terms of imprisonment. So many were they, however, that holes had to be dug for their incarceration outside the great thoroughfare of the Badaun gate, and many of the wine-bibbers died from the rigours of their confinement and others were taken out half-dead and were long in recovering their health. The terror of these holes deterred many from drinking. Those who could not give it up had to journey ten or twelve leagues [*kos*] to get a drink, for at half that distance, four or five leagues from Delhi, wine could not be publicly sold or drunk. The prevention of drinking proving very difficult, the Sultan enacted that people might distil and drink privately in their own houses, if drinking parties were not held and the liquor not sold. After the prohibition of drinking, conspiracies diminished.

Also, the Sultan commanded noblemen and great folk not to visit each other's houses, or give feasts, or hold assemblies; not to marry without royal consent, and to admit no strangers to their hospitality. Through fear of the spies, the nobles kept quiet, gave no parties, and held little intercommunication. If they went to the saraïs, they could not lay their heads together or sit down cosily and tell their troubles. So no disturbance or conspiracy arose.

The Hindu was to be so reduced as to be unable to keep a horse, wear fine clothes, or enjoy any of life's luxuries. No Hindu could hold up his head, and in their houses no sign of gold or silver or any superfluity was to be seen. These things, which nourish insubordination, were not to be found. Men looked upon revenue officers as worse than fever; to be a clerk was a crime; no man would give his daughter to such. 'Ala-ad-din was a king who had no acquaintance with learning and never associated with the learned. He considered that polity and government were one thing, and law another. "I am an unlettered man," he said [to Kazi Mughis-ad-din] "but I have seen a great deal. Be assured that the Hindus will never become submissive and obedient till they are reduced to poverty. I have therefore given orders that just enough shall be left them of corn, milk, and curds, from year to year, but that they must not accumulate hoards and property." Next day he said to him, "Although I have not studied the Science or the Book, I am a Muslim of the Muslims. To prevent rebellion, in which many perish, I issue such ordinances as I consider to be for the good of the State and the benefit of the people. Men are heedless, disregarding, and disobedient to my commands, so I have to be severe to bring them to obedience. I do not know whether this is lawful or unlawful; but whatever I think is for the good of the State or fits the emergency, that I decree."

The Sultan consulted with his most experienced ministers as to the means of reducing the prices of provisions without resorting to severe and tyrannical punishments. They replied that necessaries would never be cheap until the price of grain was fixed by tariff. Cheapness of grain is a universal benefit. So regulations were issued which kept down its price for some years. All the wise men of the age were astonished at the evenness of the price in the markets. The extraordinary part of the matter was that during the reign of 'Ala-ad-din there were years of deficient rain, but, instead of the usual scarcity ensuing, there was no lack of corn in Delhi and no rise in the price either in the royal granaries or in the dealers' importations. This was indeed the wonder of the age, and no other monarch was able to work it.

—12—

CHARACTER OF MUHAMMAD IBN TAGHLAK.

[Ibn-Batuta : *Travels.*]

Muhammad above all men delights most in giving presents and shedding blood. At his door is seen always some pauper on the way to wealth or some corpse that has been
1342. executed. Stories are rife among the people of his generosity and courage, and of his cruelty and severity. Yet he is the most humble of men and one who shows the greatest equity; the rites of religion are observed at his court; he is most strict about prayer and the punishment of those who neglect it. But his chief characteristic is generosity. Countries at some distance from India, such as the Yemen, Khorasan, Persia, are full of anecdotes of this prince, and their inhabitants know him very well: and they are not ignorant, especially, of his beneficence towards foreigners, whom he prefers to Indians and favours and honours them greatly.

He will not have them called "foreigners," for he thinks that the name must wound the heart and trouble the mind of such.

One of the grandees of India alleged that the Sultan had executed his brother without just cause, and cited him before the Kazi. The Sultan went on foot to the court, without arms, saluted, made obeisance, and stood before the Kadi whom he had notified beforehand not to rise at his entry or budge from his seat of audience. The judge gave his decision that the sovereign was bound to satisfy the plaintiff for the blood of the brother; and the decision was duly obeyed.

The Sultan was severe upon such as omitted the congregational prayers, and chastised them heavily. For this sin he executed in one day nine people, one of whom was a singer. He sent spies into the markets to punish those who were found there during prayer times, and even the men who held the horses of the servants at the gate of the hall of audience, if they missed prayers. He compelled the people to master the ordinances for ablutions, prayers, and the principles of Islam. They were examined on these matters, and if ignorant they were punished. The folk studied these things at Court and in the markets, and wrote them out. The Sultan was rigorous in the observance of the canonical law [Shari']. He abolished in 1340-1 the dues which weighed heavily on commerce, and limited taxation to the legal alms and the tenth. Every Monday and Thursday he would sit in person, with assessors, to investigate acts of oppression. No one was hindered from bringing his plea before the king. When there was such a famine in India that a maund of corn cost six dinars [three guineas], he ordered six months' food to be distributed to all the inhabitants of Delhi from the crown stores. Each person, great or small, free or slave, was to have a pound and a half Morocco weight [about 2 lbs.] a day.

In spite, however, of all that has been said about his humility, justice, goodness to the poor, and his amazing generosity, he was much given to shedding blood. It was seldom there was not a corpse at the gate of his palace. I have very often seen people killed at the gate and their bodies left there. My horse shied one day as I was going thither, and I saw a pale mass on the ground: it was a man's trunk in three pieces. This king punished little faults like great crimes; he spared neither the wise, nor the just, nor the illustrious. Each day hundreds of people were led chained into his court, their arms bound to their necks and their feet hobbled. Some were killed, others tortured or well beaten. He had the head of his own brother cut off, and the body left according to custom for three days on the ground.

One thing for which the Sultan is greatly blamed is his forcing the inhabitants of Delhi to quit their homes. The reason was that they wrote squibs and curses upon him and threw them at night into his council hall. So he resolved to ruin Delhi. He bought up the houses and sent the people to Daulatabad [Deogiri]. When they resisted, a crier went round and proclaimed that after three days not a soul must be found remaining in Delhi. Most of them went, but some hid in the houses. They were rigorously hunted out. His slaves found a cripple and a blind man in the streets and brought them before the Sultan, who had the cripple fired from a catapult and the blind man dragged to Daulatabad, a forty days' journey: he fell in pieces by the way, and only a leg arrived. All the inhabitants left, abandoning their goods and merchandise, and the city became totally deserted. A man whom I believe assured me that one evening the Sultan went up to the flat roof of his palace and gazed upon Delhi, where no fire nor smoke nor light was, and said, "Now my soul is content and my mind is at rest." Later on, he sent letters to the people of different provinces to come and repopulate the city. They ruined their own parts but did not fill Delhi, so vast, so immense is it, one of the largest cities, truly, in the world. When we arrived there we found it empty, abandoned, with only a very sparse population.

The day after our reception by the Sultan, each of us was given a horse from the royal stables, with saddle and bridle covered with ornament. The Sultan rode on a horse on entering his capital, and we did the like, riding with the advanced guard. Elephants were caparisoned in front of the king, carrying standards and sixteen parasols spangled with gold and precious stones, whilst another parasol was held over his head, and the state housing [*ghashiya*] incrusted with diamonds set in gold, was borne before him. Small catapults were mounted on some of the elephants, from which, when the Sultan drew near the city, gold and silver pieces were discharged for the crowd to scramble for. This went on till we entered the palace. Thousands walked in the procession. Kiosks of wood covered with silk for women singers were set up,

The Sultan's mother is called Mistress of the World: she is one of the best of women, most charitable, and founder of many convents [*zawiyas*] for hospitality to travellers. She is blind. Her son treats her with profound respect: once a year she travels with him, and he stays with her; when she arrives he goes to receive her, dismounts, and kisses the foot of his mother, whom all may see in her palanquin.

—13—

MUHAMMAD IBN TAGHLAK'S PROJECTS.

[Barani : *Ta'rikh-i-Firoz-Shahi.*]

Sultan Muhammad planned in his own breast three or four projects by which the whole of the habitable world was to be brought under the rule of his agents, but he never

1324-51. talked over these plans with any of his councillors or friends. Whatever he conceived he considered good, but in enforcing his schemes he lost territories, disgusted his people, and emptied his treasury. Embarrassment followed embarrassment, and confusion became worse confounded. The ill-feeling of the people gave rise to outbreaks and revolts. The rules for enforcing the royal schemes grew daily more oppressive. The tribute of most of the distant countries and provinces was lost, and many of the soldiers and servants were scattered and left in remote lands. Deficiency appeared in the treasury. The mind of the Sultan lost its balance. In the extreme weakness and harshness of his temper he abandoned himself to severity. When he found that his orders did not work so well as he wished, he became yet more embittered against his people. He cut them down like weeds, and punished them. He devised oppressive taxes [in the Doab] and made stoppages from the land-revenues till the backs of the rayats were broken. Those who were rich became rebels ; the lands were ruined and cultivation was arrested. Grain became dear, the rains were deficient, so famine became general. It lasted for years, and thousands upon thousands of people perished.

Another plan which was ruinous was making Deogiri the capital, with the title of Daulatabad. It had a central situation, nearly equidistant from Delhi, Gujarat, Lakhnauti, Tilang, and other chief places. Without consultation or weighing the *pros* and *cons*, he brought ruin on Delhi which for 170 or 180 years had grown in prosperity and rivalled Baghdad and Cairo. The city, with its saraïs and suburbs and villages, spread over four or five leagues: all was destroyed. Not a cat or a dog was left. Troops of the inhabitants with their families were forced to remove, broken-hearted; many perished on the road, and those who reached Deogiri, unable to endure their exile, pined to death. All round Deogiri, an infidel land, spread graveyards of Muslims. The Sultan was bounteous to the emigrants, both on the journey and arrival; but they were tender and could not suffer the exile. They laid down their heads in that heathen land, and of their multitudes few lived to return to their native home.

A third project also did great havoc: this was the issue of copper money to be used as [standard] currency, like gold and silver. This edict turned the house of every Hindu into a mint, and the Indians of the provinces coined krors and lacs of copper coins, with which they paid their tribute and bought horses and arms and fine things of all sorts. The raïs, the village headmen, and landowners grew rich on these copper coins, but the State was impoverished. In no long time distant countries would only accept the copper tanka as metal, and in places where reverence for the edict prevailed the gold tanka rose to be worth a hundred copper tankas. Every goldsmith struck copper coins in his workshop, and the treasury was crammed with them. They fell so low, that they were counted no more valuable than pebbles or potsherds. Trade being disrupted, the Sultan repealed his edict, and in great wrath proclaimed that all the copper coins would be redeemed in gold or silver at the treasury. Thousands brought them for exchange and their heaps rose up in Taghlakabad like mountains.

—14—

THE PLENTEOUS REIGN OF FIROZ SHAH.

[Shams-i-Siraj Afif: *Ta'rikh-i-Firoz-Shahi.*]

By the blessing of God favourable seasons and abundance of the necessaries of life prevailed in the reign of Firoz Shah, not only in the capital, but throughout his dominions. During the whole forty years of his reign there was no appearance of scarcity, and the times were so happy that the people of Delhi forgot the reign of 'Ala-ad-din although no more prosperous times than his had ever fallen to the lot of any Muhammadan sovereign. 'Ala-ad-din took such pains to keep down the price of the necessaries of life that his exertions have found a record in famous histories. To the merchants he gave wealth, and placed before them goods in abundance and gold without measure. He showed them every kingly favour, and fixed on them regular salaries. In the reign of 'Ala-ad-din the necessaries of life were abundant through excellent management; but through the favour of God, grain continued cheap throughout the reign of Firoz Shah, without any effort on his part. Grain was so cheap that in the city of Delhi wheat was eight *jitals* a *maund* and grain and barley four *jitals*. A camp follower could give his horse a feed of ten *sirs* [20 lbs.] of corn for one *jital*. Fabrics of all kinds were cheap, and silk goods, both white and coloured, were of moderate price. Orders were given for the reduction of the price of sweetmeats in accord with the general fall of prices.

1351-88.

Sultan Firoz had a great taste for the laying out of gardens, which he took great pains to beautify. He made twelve hundred gardens round Delhi and restored thirty which had been begun by 'Ala-ad-din. Near Salaura he made eighty gardens, and forty-four in Chitor. In all of them were white and black grapes of seven varieties, and the government share of the garden produce came to 80,000 *tankas*, after deducting what was paid to owners and gardeners. The revenues of the Doab in this reign amounted to eighty lacs of *tankas*; and under the fostering care of this religious sovereign, the revenues of the territories of Delhi were six krors and eighty-five lacs of *tankas* [60,850,000]. The Sultan throughout his reign, in his great sagacity and prudence, endeavoured to circumscribe the extent of his dominions, but still the revenues amounted to the sum stated. All this large revenue was duly appointed out; each Khan received a sum suitable to his exalted position; the amirs and maliks also obtained allowances according to their dignity, and the officials were paid enough to provide a comfortable living. The soldiers of the army received grants of land [jagirs] enough to support them in comfort, and the irregulars received payment from the government treasury. Those soldiers who did not receive their pay in this manner were, according to their necessity, supplied with assignments upon the revenues. When these assignments of the soldiers arrived in the fiefs, the holders used to get about half the total amount from the holders of the fiefs. It was the practice of certain persons in those days to buy up these assignments, which was an accommodation to both parties. They used to give one-third of the value for them in the city, and receive one-half in the districts. The purchasers of these assignments carried on a traffic in them, and gaining a good profit, many of them got rich and made their fortunes.

Sultan Firoz, under divine inspiration, spread all the revenues of his territories among his people. The various districts of the fiefs were also divided. Khan-i-Jahan, the vazir, exclusive of the allowances for his retainers, friends, and sons, received a sum of thirteen lacs of tankas, or instead of it sundry fiefs and districts. Other chiefs were similarly provided for, according to their merit; some receiving eight lacs of tankas, others six lacs and others four lacs. All the khans and maliks grew rich in his reign, and had vast stores of wealth and jewels and diamonds of great value. When Malik Shahin Shahna, who was naib-amir of the Majlis-i-khass, died and his effects were examined, a sum of fifty lacs of tankas, in cash, was taken out of his house, besides horses, valuables, and jewels in abundance. The Sultan being thus beneficent, all men, high and low, were devoted to him.

—15—

TIMUR MASSACRES THE HINDU PRISONERS.

[*"Autobiography"*: *Malfusat-i-Timuri.*]

From the time of entering Hindustan up to the present we had taken more than 100,000 infidels and Hindus prisoners, and they were all now in my camp. On the previous day, when the enemy made an attack upon us, the prisoners made signs of rejoicing, cursed us, and were ready, should they hear of the enemy's success, to collect, break their bonds, plunder our tents, and then join the enemy and thus increase his strength. I asked my amirs' advice, and they said that on the great day of battle these 100,000 prisoners could not be left with the baggage and that it would be entirely opposed to the rules of war to set them free. In fact no other course remained but to make them all food for the sword. When I heard these words, I found them consonant with the rules of war, and immediately gave

1398.

my command for the Tawachis to proclaim throughout the camp that every man who had infidel prisoners was to put them to death, on pain of being himself executed and his property confiscated to the informer. When this order reached the warriors of Islam, they drew their swords and put their prisoners to death. One hundred thousand infidels, impious idolaters, were that day slain. A counsellor and man of learning, who in all his life had never killed a sparrow, now in execution of my order slew with his own sword fifteen Hindus, his captives.

—16—

TIMUR'S VICTORY BY THE JUMNA.

[Yazdi: *Zafar-nama.*]

The enemy's army consisted of 12,000 veteran horsemen and 40,000 infantry, with all the apparatus of war. His chief reliance was on his 120 enormous war-elephants,
1398. who were plated with armour and carried crossbowmen and disk-throwers in litters on their backs. Sharp poisoned points were fitted to their tusks, and rocket-men and grenade-throwers marched beside them. The army of Timur was weak compared with the Indians, but his troops did not rate their enemy very highly; yet though they had fought in many a battle and overthrown many a foe, they had never so far encountered elephants and had heard terrible stories of their powers. When Timur apportioned the posts for the various officers of the Court and courteously desired the learned doctors of the law who accompanied the invasion to tell him where they would like to be placed, they answered, terrified by tales about the elephants, "Along with the ladies."

To allay his men's fears he ordered them to fix palisades and dig a trench in front of the army, and tethered buffaloes, firmly fastened together with thongs, in front of the palisade, and distributed claws [caltrops] to throw on the ground before the elephants. Heaven always favoured Timur and now gave him success without the aid of any of these devices. He mounted a hillock between the two armies and reconnoitred all round. After viewing the opposing forces, he dismounted from his horse and turning to heaven the face of supplication he offered up his prayer for victory. It was not long before its acceptance was signified. Reinforcements having been sent to the support of the right wing and the vanguard, these manœuvres so cheered the spirits and braced the courage of the men that they drew their swords and charged the enemy furiously. The elephants, huge of form and craven of spirit, stampeded, and thus Timur won the day. His men had cut their way to the elephants, killed their drivers, and wounded the trunks with swords and arrows. The soldiers of India fought bravely for their lives, but the frail insect cannot contend against the raging wind nor the feeble deer against the fierce lion; so they were forced to flee.

—17—

SACK OF DELHI.

[Yazdi: *Zafar-nama.*]

On the 16th a number of soldiers collected at the gate of Delhi and mocked the inhabitants. When Timur heard of it
1398. he sent some amirs to stop it; but it was the divine pleasure to ruin the city and punish its people. It happened thus. Some ladies went into the city to see the

Palace of a Thousand Columns which Malik Jauna had built in Jahanpanah; officers of the treasury had also entered to collect the indemnity; and several thousand soldiers, with requisitions for grain and sugar, had gone too. Their officers had orders to arrest every nobleman who had fought against Timur and taken refuge in Delhi. When parties of soldiers were thus going about the city, numbers of Hindus and infidels in the cities of Delhi, Siri, Jahanpanah, and Old Delhi, seeing their violence, took up arms and attacked them. Many others set fire to their goods and threw their wives and children and themselves on the flames. The soldiers waxed the more eager for plunder and destruction. Bold as the striving Hindus were, the officers in charge kept the gates shut and allowed no more troops to enter; but there were some 15,000 men already in, busy all that Friday night in pillaging and burning the houses, and in the morning the soldiers outside broke in and added to the tumult. The whole place was sacked, and several palaces in Jahanpanah and Siri destroyed. This plundering went on through the 18th. Every soldier got more than twenty slaves, and some brought fifty or a hundred men, women, and children, as slaves out of the city, besides spoils of money, jewellery, and gold and silver plate beyond computation. On the 19th Old Delhi was remembered, where many Hindus had taken refuge in the great mosque, prepared to defend their lives. Two amirs with 500 trusty men were sent against them and falling on them with the sword despatched them to hell. Towers were built high with their heads, and their bodies were left to the beasts and birds of prey. On that day all Old Delhi was sacked. Such inhabitants as escaped death were made prisoners. Several thousand craftsmen were brought out and distributed by Timur among the princes and officers; the stonemasons were reserved to build for the conqueror a great mosque at his capital, Samarkand.

— 18 —

'ALA-AD-DIN BAHMANI.

[Firishta.]

To every part of his dominions he sent censors of morals and just judges; and though he drank wine himself, he forbade it to others, as also gaming. He put chains
1435. on the necks of idle vagabonds and made them street scavengers and labourers, that they might reform and earn their livelihood, or else quit the country. If any one, of any rank, after warning and moderate correction, was convicted of drinking, melted lead was to be poured down his throat.

— 19 —

HUMAYUN BAHMANI.

[Firishta.]

Humayun Shah, abandoning himself to the full indulgence of his cruel propensities and mad with rage, caused stakes to be set up on each side of the royal market and
1458. vicious elephants and wild beasts to be placed in the square, and cauldrons of scalding oil and boiling water for torture. Looking on from a balcony, he had his brother Hasan thrown to a ferocious tiger who tore him to pieces and devoured him. Ingenious tortures were invented by the King and inflicted on young and old of both sexes. About seven thousand persons, including women and servants who had no connection with the late rebellion, were killed in various savage ways. He put the women servants of his household to death for the most trivial faults; and when any of the nobility were obliged to wait upon him, so great was their dread that they took a last leave of their families.

—20—

SULTAN BAHLOL LODI.

['Abdallah: *Ta'rikh-i-Daüdi.*]

Bahlol was indeed a King who fostered religion and showed courage and generosity. Mercy and benevolence were habitual with him, and he was a great respecter
1451-88. of law. He spent much time in the company of learned and holy men, and devoted himself to administering justice and hearing the petitions of his subjects and he did not leave them to his ministers' disposal: he never turned away a suppliant. He gathered in treasure and conducted himself without ostentation; he never sat on a throne or made his nobles stand in his presence. He maintained a brotherly intercourse with his chiefs and soldiers; if anyone were ill, he would himself go and attend on him. He was brave to a fault, and on a day of battle, as soon as he saw the enemy, he would dismount and fall on his knees to pray for the success of Islam and the safety of the Muslims, and to acknowledge his own powerlessness. From the day he became king, none ever won a victory from him, nor did he once leave a stricken field till he had won the day, unless he was carried off wounded. Else, he avoided an engagement from the first.

He was at worship in the great mosque in the first week of his accession, and Mulla Fazin, who read the khutba, came down from the pulpit and said, "God be praised, we have an amazing tribe to rule us; whether they are servants of the devil or devils themselves I know not; but their [Afghan] language is so barbarous that they call a mother *mur*, a brother *rur*, a nurse *shur*, a soldier *tur*, and a man *nur*!" Sultan Bahlol put his handkerchief to his mouth, and then cried, laughing, "Enough, Mulla Fazin! Hold! We are all servants of God."

— 21 —

SULTAN SIKANDAR LODI.

['Abdallah: *Ta'rikh-i-Daüdi.*]

Sultan Sikandar was a most illustrious monarch, famed for liberality, honour, and politeness, inwardly pious and outwardly handsome, very religious towards God and
1488-1518. to his people benevolent; just and courageous, his equity beheld the weak and the strong with the same eye, and he was continually balancing evidence, deciding suits, and trying to make his subjects happy. He remained awake all night whilst he heard the petitions of the poor, regulated the affairs of the kingdom, and ordered the issue of firmans and letters. Seventeen learned and accomplished men were always with him, and after midnight he would call for food, and these seventeen learned men would wash their hands and seat themselves in front of him. Dishes were brought in and the Sultan ate, but though food was also set before the seventeen learned men they were not allowed to touch it. When the King had finished, they carried off their plates to their houses and ate there. Some say his Majesty, to keep his health, secretly drank wine.

Every business had its appointed time and a custom once fixed was never changed. When the Sultan had once allowed a particular meat or drink he never altered it. A man of note came from Jaunpur to visit him in the hot weather and was given six jars of sherbet with his food on account of the heat and thirst; but when he came again in winter he still had six jars of sherbet to drink. The Sultan always behaved to the nobles and great men in exactly the same way after many years as he did on the first day. His conversation was controlled and never desultory. He had a retentive memory. In his reign business was pursued in a peaceful, honest, straightforward way. Life took a new shape, for all were courteous and self-respecting, and integrity and piety prevailed as never before; nor were literature, medicine, and industries neglected.

— 22 —

BABUR WELCOMES HIS COUSIN MIRZA HAIDAR.

[Mirza Haidar: *Ta'rikh-i-Rashidi.*

Trans: E. Denison Ross.]

When I came into his presence [at Kabul], the joy-diffusing glance of the Emperor fell upon me, and from the excess of his love and the intensity of his kindness, strong pearls and rubies began to rain down upon me from his benign jewel-scattering eye. He extended to me the hand of favour and bade me welcome. He then clasped me to the bosom of affection, drew me to the breast of fatherly love, and held me there for a while. When he let me go, he would no longer allow me to observe the formalities of respect, but made me sit down at his side. While we were thus seated, he said to me with great benevolence: "Your father and brother and all your relations have been made to drink the wine of martyrdom; but, thank God, you have come back to me again in safety. Do not grieve too much at their loss. For I will take their place, and whatever favour of affection you could have expected from them, this, and more, will I show you."

I passed a long time in the service of the Emperor, in perfect happiness and freedom from care; and he was for ever, by promises of kindness or by threats of severity, encouraging me to study. If he ever noticed any little virtue or new acquisition, he would praise it in the highest terms, commend it to everybody, and invite their approbation. At that time the Emperor showed me such affection and kindness as a fond father shows his son and heir. From this time to the year 918 I remained in his service.
1512. Whenever he rode out, I had the honour of riding at his side, and when he received friends I was sure to be among the invited. In fact, he never let me be separated from him.

—23—

BABUR'S RESOLVE TO INVADE INDIA.

[Babur's *Memoirs.*]

It was at last determined in council to make a move on Hindustan. In the month of Sha'ban [910 H., Jan. 1505] when the sun was in Aquarius we rode out from
1505. Kabul for Hindustan, and in six marches reached Adinapur. I had never before seen a hot country nor the borderland of Hindustan. In Ningnahar I beheld a new world, other grasses, other trees, other animals, other birds, other manners and customs of the nomad tribes. We were amazed, and truly there was room for wonder.

From the time when I conquered the country of Kabul in 1504 I had always been bent on Hindustan. The hesitation of my Begs, who disliked the plan, and the cabals and opposition of my brothers prevented me and the Indian provinces escaped being overrun. At length these obstacles were removed and there was none left who could oppose. In 925 [1519] we led out an army, and having taken Bajaur by storm, in 2-3 *ghâri*, and massacring its people, we went on into Bhira, where we neither overran nor plundered, but imposed an indemnity upon the inhabitants, divided the money among the troops, and returned to Kabul. From then till [1526] we devotedly held tight to Hindustan and entered it five times at the head of an army. The fifth time, God Most High of his grace and mercy cast down and defeated an enemy so mighty as Sultan Ibrahim, and made Hindustan our conquest and possession.

—24—

CROSSING THE MOUNTAINS.

[Babur's *Memoirs.*]

For about a week we went on trampling down the snow, yet only able to make two or three miles a day. I helped

1507. in trampling the snow; with ten or fifteen of my household, and with Kasim Beg and his sons and a few servants, we all dismounted and laboured at beating down the snow. Each step we sank to the waist or the breast, but still we went on trampling it down. After a few paces a man became exhausted, and another took his place. Then the men who were treading it down dragged forward a horse without a rider; the horse sank to the stirrups and girths, and after advancing ten or fifteen paces was worn out and replaced by another; and thus from ten to twenty of us trod down the snow and brought our horses on, whilst the rest—even our best men, many of them Begs—rode along the road thus beaten down for them, hanging their heads. It was no time for worrying them or using authority: if a man has pluck and hardihood, he will press forward to such work of his own accord.

That night the storm was terrible and snow fell so heavily that we all expected to die together. When we reached the mountain-cave the storm was at its worst. We dismounted at its mouth. Deep snow! a one-man road! and even on that stamped-down and trampled road, pitfalls for horses! the days at their shortest! The first arrivals reached the cave by daylight; later, they dismounted wherever they happened to be; dawn found many still in the saddle. The cave seemed small. I took a shovel, and scraping and clearing the snow away made a place for myself as big as a prayer-carpet near its mouth. I dug down breast high, but did not reach the ground. This made me a little shelter from the wind when I sat right down in it. They begged me to go inside, but I would not. I felt that for me to be in warm shelter and comfort whilst my men were out in the snow and drift,—for me to be sleeping at ease inside whilst my men were in misery and distress,—was not a man's act, and far from comradeship. What strong men can stand, I would stand: for, as the Persian proverb says, "In the company of friends, Death is a nuptial feast." So I remained sitting in the snow and wind in the hole that I had dug out, with snow four hands thick on my head and back and ears.

— 25 —

BABUR IN HIS HOURS OF EASE.

[Babur's *Memoirs.*]

[Oct. 14.] Next day I went to the Garden of Fulfilment. It was the season of its beauty. Its lawns were a sheet of
1519. trefoil; its pomegranate trees were yellowed to autumn splendour; it was their season, and the fruit hung red on the trees. The orange trees were green and bright with countless oranges, but the best were not yet ripe. I never was so delighted as now with the Garden of Fulfilment.

[Oct. 18.] We halted at Jagdalik. Towards evening prayer there was a drinking party; most of the household were present. Near the end, Gedai Muhammad grew very noisy and troublesome, and when he got drunk slid down on the cushion by my side, whereupon Gedai Taghai picked him up and carried him out. Marching thence before daybreak I explored the valley of the Barik-ab: some *turak* trees were in great beauty. We halted there and having dined seasonably we drank wine in honour of the rich crop. We made them kill a sheep picked up on the road, had some meat dressed, and amused ourselves by kindling oak branches.

[Oct. 29.] On Sunday I had a party in the small Picture-cabinet over the gate. Though the room is very small we were sixteen. [30th.] We went to Istalif to see the harvest. This day was done the sin of *ma'jun* [*i.e.* I took *bhang*]. During the night there was a great deal of rain: most of the Begs and household were obliged to take refuge in my tent outside the garden. Next morning we had a drinking party in the same garden: we continued at it till night. On the following morning [1 November] we again had an early cup and, getting intoxicated, went to sleep. About noonday prayers we left Istalif and took a drug [*bhang*] on the road. It was about afternoon prayers before we reached Bihzadi. The crops were extremely good. While we were riding round the harvest fields, those who were fond of wine began to contrive another drinking bout. Although *bhang* had been taken, yet, as the crops were uncommonly fine, we sat down under some trees that had yielded a plentiful load of fruit, and began to drink. We kept up the party in the same place till bedtime prayers. 'Abdallah, who had got very drunk and made an offensive remark, recovering his senses, was in terrible perturbation, and conversed in a wonderfully smooth and sweet strain all the rest of the evening.

[Jan. 6.] We embarked on a raft and alighted near the Garden of Fulfilment. Its oranges were yellowing well and the
1520. green of the plants was beautiful. We stayed five or six days there. As I intended when forty years old to abstain from wine, and as now I wanted somewhat less than one year of that age, I drank wine most copiously. [Jan. 7.] Mulla Yarak played an air which he composed to the *mukhammas* measure: while I took my drug. It was charming. For some time I had not much attended to musical matters. I took a fancy that I too should compose something. [10th.] While taking an early glass it was said in sport that whoever spoke like a Persian should drink a cup. In the result, many drank. About nine in the morning, while we were sitting under the willows in the meadow, it was proposed that everyone who spoke like a Turk should drink a cup; and numbers drank. When the sun mounted high we went under the orange trees and drank our wine on the bank.

—26—

SIEGE OF BAJAUR.

[Babur's *Memoirs.*]

The people of Bajaur had never seen matchlocks and at first were not in the least afraid of them, but, hearing the sound of shots, stood in front of the guns, mocking and play-
1519. ing derisive antics. But Ustad 'Ali Kuli brought down five men, and Wali the Treasurer two, and the other matchlockmen shot well and bravely, through shield, mail, and *Kusaru* [cowhead?] [penthouses]; so that before night seven to ten Bajauris were laid low; whereupon the defenders of the fort grew so frightened that not a man ventured to show his head. As it was now evening the troops were ordered to draw off and prepare implements and engines for an assault at dawn.

On Friday, 5th Muharram [7 Jan.], at the first streak of light the drum was sounded for the troops to move forward to their stations and scale the place. The left and centre, bringing their *tura* [mantelet] advanced, and set up scaling ladders and began to climb. Dost Beg's men reached the foot of a north-east tower and began undermining and destroying the wall. Ustad 'Ali Kuli was there too, and again worked his matchlock to good purpose; the *Firingi* [European] gun was twice discharged. At the left of the centre Malik 'Ali, having scaled the wall by a ladder, was engaged hand to hand with the enemy; in the lines of the main body, Muhammad 'Ali Jangjang and his younger brother Nauroz, each scaling up a ladder, fought bravely with sword and spear; while Baba the waitingman [Yasawal], on top of another ladder, was hacking at the parapet with his axe. Many of our men climbed up boldly and plied the enemy with arrows till never a head was shown; others broke through the walls and demolished the defences. By breakfast time the N. E. tower, undermined by Dost Beg, was breached, the enemy driven in, and the tower captured. At the same time the main body scaled the walls and entered the fort. By God's favour this strong castle was taken in two or three hours.

—27—

BATTLE OF PANIPAT.

[Bahur's *Memoirs.*]

At our next camp it was ordered that every man should collect carts. Seven hundred carts were brought in, and the
1526. order to Ustad 'Ali Kuli was that these carts should be joined together in the Ottoman fashion, but with twisted thongs instead of chains, and that between every two, five or six mantelets should be fixed, behind which the matchlockmen were to stand to fire. We halted five or six days in this camp to get these collected and set up. Then the Begs and men of experience and knowledge were called together to a general council. It was decided that Panipat, with its crowded houses, would cover our flank, while we would fortify our front by mantelets and carts, in the rear of which the foot matchlockmen would stand. This resolved, we moved and in two marches reached Panipat [12 April]. On our right were the town and suburbs; in front the carts and mantelets already prepared; on the left we dug trenches and made obstacles with the boughs of trees. At the interval of every bowshot a gap was left wide enough to let a hundred or a hundred and fifty men sally through. Many of the troops

were in great trepidation, and it was no reproach to them: they had come two or three months' journey from their homes; we had to engage a strange people, whose language we did not understand nor they ours; the army opposed to us was estimated at 100,000 men; the elephants of the emperor and his officers were said to number nearly 1,000. He had the hoarded treasures of his predecessors, in current coin ready to hire more troops. But God Almighty guided everything for the best. Sultan Ibrahim had not the heart to satisfy his men or part with his treasure. He was an unproved youth; he was negligent in all his movements, he marched without order, retired or halted without plan, and engaged in battle without foresight. [20 April.] By the time of the first morning prayer, on Friday, 8th Rajab, when the light was such that you could distinguish objects, notice was brought from the patrols that the enemy were advancing in order of battle. We too immediately braced on our armour and mounted. The right division was led by Humayun [etc.], the left by Muhammad Sultan Mirza [etc.]. Chin Timur and Khalifa commanded the right and the left of the centre. Khusrau Gokultash led the advance; 'Abd-al-'Aziz, the Master of the Horse, commanded the reserve. There was stationed a turning party of Moguls by the right and the left division with orders, when the enemy were near enough, to make a circuit and take them in the rear.

When the dark mass of the enemy first came in sight they seemed to press chiefly against the right; so it was reinforced from 'Abd-al-Aziz's reserves. Sultan Ibrahim's army never made a halt but came straight on at a quick march. But when they got near and viewing my troops saw them drawn up in the order and with the defences that have been described, they were brought to a stand for a while, hesitating. They could not stand nor yet advance with the same speed as before. Our orders were for the turning parties on the extremes of the right and left divisions to wheel round the enemy's flank with the utmost speed and instantly attack them in the rear; while the right and left divisions were to charge. Mahdi Khwaja came up before the rest of the left wing, and a body of men with an elephant faced him, but were driven back at last by sharp volleys of arrows. I sent Ahmadi the Secretary from the main body to support the left. The battle was also obstinate on the right. I ordered Muhammad Gokultash and others to engage those in front of the centre. Ustad 'Ali Kuli sed his *Firingi* guns to good purpose many times in front of the centre, and Mustafa, the cannoneer, on the left centre, worked his artillery with great execution.

The right and left divisions, centre and turners, having now surrounded the enemy, were hard at work pouring arrows upon them. The enemy made one or two weak charges on the right and left, but our men plied them with arrows and drove them in upon their centre, so that huddled together and in confusion the enemy could neither advance nor flee.

The sun had mounted spear-high when the onset began, and the battle lasted till midday; noon passed, the enemy were routed and broken and our friends victorious and exulting. By the grace and mercy of Almighty God, this arduous task was made easy for us and this mighty army in the space of half a day was laid in the dust. Five or six thousand men were found lying slain in one spot near Ibrahim. We reckoned that the slain in different parts of the battlefield numbered 15,000 or 16,000 men; but it came out later in Agra from the accounts of the natives that 40,000 or 50,000 had fallen in this field. After routing the enemy, we continued the pursuit, slaughtering and making prisoners.

— 28 —

BABUR RENOUNCES WINE.

[Babur's *Memoirs.*]

I had mounted to inspect my outposts, and in the course of my ride I was seriously struck by the reflection that I had
1527. always resolved at sometime or other to make an effectual repentance, and that my sins had set a lasting stain upon my heart. I said to myself, O my soul—

How long wilt thou draw savour from sin?
Repentance is not unpalatable—taste it.
How great has been thy defilement from sin?
How much peace has transgression given?
How long hast thou been the slave of thy passions!
How much of thy life hast thou flung away!
Since thou hast set out on a Holy War,
Thou hast seen death before thine eyes.
Whoso resolves to sacrifice his life to save it
Shall attain that state which thou knowest,
Removing him far from forbidden joys,
Cleansing him from all offences.
With my own gain before me, I vowed to obey,
In this my Transgression, the drinking of wine.

The flagons and cups of silver and gold, the goblets of feasting,
I had them all brought;
I had them all broken up then and there.
Thus eased I my heart by renouncement of wine.

The fragments of the gold and silver vessels were distributed among the deserving and the poor.

—29—

BABUR'S ADDRESS TO TROOPS BEFORE BATTLE OF KANWAHA.

[Babur's *Memoirs.*]

1527. Observing the discouragement of my troops and their want of spirit, I formed my plan. I called an assembly of all the Begs and officers and addressed them :—

Gentlemen and soldiers.—" Every man that cometh into the world must pass away. God alone is immortal, unchangeable. Whose sitteth down to the feast of life must end by drinking the cup of death. He who hath come to the inn of life must one day leave this house of woe." Rather let us die with honour than live disgraced.

'With fame, though I die, I am content;
Let fame be mine, though life be spent.'

God most High has been gracious in giving us this happiness and fortune, that if we fall we die martyrs ; if we conquer we triumph in his cause. Let each of us swear upon his Holy Word that he will never turn back from this foe, nor shrink from the stress of battle, so long as life remains in his body.

All present, master and servant, great and small, eagerly seized the blessed Koran and took the oath.

—30—

SHIR KHAN'S RESOLVE.

['Abbas Khan : *Ta'rikh-i-Shir-Shahi.*]

I, 'Abbas, the writer of the adventures of Shir Khan, have heard from the mouth of Shaikh Muhammad mine own uncle,

whose age was near eighty years, the following story: "I was at the battle of Chanderi with the army of Babur.
1527. Shaikh Ibrahim Sarwani said to me, 'Come to Shir Khan's quarters and hear his impossible boastings which all men are laughing at.' Accordingly we rode over to Shir Khan's quarters. In the course of conversation Shaikh Ibrahim said, 'It is impossible that empire should again fall into the hands of the Afghans and the Moguls be expelled from the country.' Shir Khan replied, 'Shaikh Muhammad, be you witness now between Shaikh Ibrahim and myself that if fortune favour me I will very shortly expel the Moguls from Hind; for the Moguls are not superior to the Afghans in battle or man to man, but the Afghans have let the empire of Hind slip from their hands by their divisions. Since I have been amongst the Moguls and know their bearing in action, I see that they have no order or discipline, and that their kings from pride do not themselves conduct the government but leave all affairs of state to their nobles and ministers, trusting them fully in word and act. But these grandees act on corrupt motives in every case; whether it be that of soldier or cultivator or rebellious zamindar, whoever, whether loyal or disloyal, has money, can get his business settled to his task by paying for it; but the man without money, though he has shown loyalty on a hundred occasions and be a veteran in arms, will never gain his end. For desire for gold they do not distinguish between friend and foe; and if luck attends me the Shaikh shall soon see how I will bring the Afghans under my sway and never again let them become divided.'"

—31—

CHARACTER OF HUMAYUN.

[Mirza Haidar: *Ta'rikh-i-Rashidi.*
Trans. Ross.]

Humayun Padishah was the eldest, greatest, and most renowned of Babur's sons. I have seen few persons possessed of so much natural talent and excellence as he; but in consequence of frequent intercourse with the sensual and profligate men who served him, he had contracted some bad habits; among these was his addiction to opium. All the evil that has been set down to the emperor, and has become the common talk of the people, is attributable to this vice. Nevertheless, he was endowed with excellent qualities, being brave in battle, gay in feast, and very generous. In short, he was a dignified, stately sovereign, who observed much state and pomp. When I entered his service at Agra, it was after his defeats and people said that, compared with what had been, there was nothing left of his pomp and magnificence.
1539. Yet when his army was arrayed for the Ganges campaign (in which the whole direction devolved upon me), there were still 17,000 menials in his retinue, from which circumstance an estimate may be formed of the rest of his establishment.

The emperor and myself had become friends after the Mogul fashion, and he had given me the name of *dast* [friend]. In council he never addressed me by any other name, and on the firmans it was written in this manner. No one of my brothers or the Sultans of the time, who had been in the Emperor's service, had ever been honoured in such a way as was I, Muhammad Haidar Kurkan, who, being the approved friend of such a prince as the Emperor, was not only called "brother" but was chosen as *dast.*

—32—

THE BEGAMS AT AGRA.

[Gul-badan's *Memoirs.*
Trans. Mrs. A. S. Beveridge.]

On Court days, which were Sundays and Tuesdays, the Emperor used to go to the other side of the river. During his

1535. stay in the garden my mother and sisters and the ladies were often in his company. . . . All of us, the begams and my sisters were in his society; when he went to any begam's or sister's quarters, all the begams and all his sisters used to go with him. Next day he came to the tent of this lowly person [his sister Gul-badan], and the entertainment lasted till the third watch of the night. Many begams were there, and his sisters, and ladies of rank and of position, and other ladies, and musicians and reciters. After the third watch, his Majesty was pleased to command repose. His sisters and the begams made resting places in his presence [slept where they were].

Bega Begam woke us up and said, "It is time for prayers." His Majesty ordered water for ablution made ready where he was. So the begam knew that he was awake. She began a complaint, and said to him, "For several days now you have been paying visits in this garden, and on no one day have you been to our house. Thorns have not been planted in the way to it. We hope you will deign to visit our quarters also and to have a party and a sociable gathering there, too. How long will you continue to show all these disfavours to us helpless ones? We too have hearts. Three times you have honoured other places by visits, and you have run day and night into one in amusement and conversation."

When she had finished, his Majesty said nothing and went to prayers. At the first watch he came out and sent for [us]. . . . Then after a little he began, "Bibi, what ill treatment at my hands did you complain of this morning?" and "That was not the place to make a complaint. You all know that I have been to the quarters of the elder relations of you all. It is a necessity laid on me to make them happy. Nevertheless I am ashamed before them because I see them so rarely. It has long been in my mind to ask you for a signed declaration, and it is as well that you have brought me to the speaking point. I am an opium eater. If there should be delay in my comings and goings, do not be angry with me. Rather, write me a letter and say, 'Whether it please you to come or not, we are content and are thankful to you.'"

Gul-barg Begam wrote to that effect at once and he settled it with her. Bega Begam insisted a little saying, "The excuse looked worse than the fault. . ." She wrote the letter to him.

—33—

BATTLE OF THE GANGES.

[Mirza Haidar: *Ta'rikh-i-Rashidi*.
Trans. Ross.]

The Imperial army reached the banks of the Ganges in the best way that it could. There it lay encamped for about a
1540. month, the Emperor being on one side of the river and Shir Khan on the other, facing each other. The armies may have amounted to more than 200,000 men. Among the equipments which were in the train of the Emperor were 700 carriages, each drawn by four pairs of bullocks

and carrying a swivel which discharged a ball of 500 *miskals'* weight. I myself saw several times that from the top of an eminence they unfailingly struck horsemen who slightly and unsuspectingly exposed themselves. And there were 21 carriages each drawn by eight pairs of bullocks. Stone balls were of no use in them, but the shots were of molten brass weighing 5,000 *miskals*, and the cost of each was 200 *miskals* of silver. They would strike anything that was visible at the distance of a parasang.

Everybody began to desert, and the most surprising part of it was that many of those who deserted did not go over to Shir Khan, and so could expect no favour from him. An excited feeling ran through the army, and the cry was, "Let us go and rest in our homes." As the army had taken to desert, it was judged better to risk a battle than to see it go to ruin without fighting. If the result were unfavourable, we could not, at least, be accused of having abandoned an empire like Hindustan without striking a blow. Another consideration was that if we passed the river, desertion would no longer be possible. We therefore crossed over.

On the 10th Muharram, 947 H., we mounted to carry our plan into effect and made our dispositions. As had been determined, the carriages and mortars and small guns were placed in the centre. The command of the guns was given to Muhammad Khan Rumi, to the sons of Ustad 'Ali Kuli, to Ustad Ahmad Rumi, and Husain Khalifa. They placed the carriages and mortars in their proper positions [in front, and the gunners, nearly 5,000 in number], and stretched chains between them. In other divisions there were amirs of no repute.

The Emperor had posted the author of this book upon his left, so that his right flank should be on the Emperor's left. In the same position he had placed a force of chosen troops.

On my left all my retainers were stationed. I had 400 chosen men, inured to warfare and familiar with battle, fifty of whom were mounted on horses accoutred with armour. Between me and the river there was a force of twenty-seven amirs, all of whom carried the *tugh* [banner]. In this position also were the other components of the left wing, and they must be judged of by the others: — on the day of battle, when Shir Khan, having formed his divisions, marched out, of all these twenty-seven banners not one was to be seen, for the great nobles had hidden them in the apprehension that the enemy might advance upon them. The soldiership and bravery of the amirs may be conceived from this exhibition of courage.

Shir Khan came out in five divisions of 1,000 men each, and in advance of him were 3,000 men. I estimated the whole as being less than 15,000, but I calculated the Chaghatai [Mogul] force at about 40,000, all mounted on *tipchak* horses, and clad in iron armour. They surged like the waves of the sea, but the courage of the amirs and officers of the army was such as I have described. When Shir Khan's army came out of its entrenchments, two divisions, which seemed to be equal to four divisions, drew up in that place, and three divisions advanced against their opponents. On our side I was leading the centre to take up the position which I had selected; but when we reached the ground, we were unable to occupy it, for every amir and vazir in the Chaghatai army, whether he is rich or poor, has his camp-followers [*ghulams*]. An amir of note, with his hundred retainers and followers, has five hundred servants and *ghulams*, who on the day of battle render no assistance to their masters and have no control over themselves. So in whatever place there was a conflict the *ghulams* were entirely ungovernable. When they lost their masters, they were seized with panic and blindly rushed about in terror.

In short, it was impossible to hold our ground. They so pressed us in the rear that they drove the centre upon the chains stretched between the chariots, and they and the soldiers dashed each other upon them. Those who were behind so pressed upon those who were in front that they broke through the chains. The men who were posted by the chains were driven beyond them, and the few who remained behind were broken, so that all formation was destroyed.

Such was the state of the centre. On the right, Shir Khan advanced in battle array; but, before an arrow was discharged, the camp followers fled like chaff before the wind, and, breaking the line, they all pressed towards the centre. The *ghulams*, whom the commander had sent to the front, rushed to the lines of chariots, and the whole array was broken: the Mir was separated from his men, and the men from the Mir. When the centre was thus broken, all the fugitives from the right bore down upon it. I had estimated the Chaghatai army as numbering 40,000 men, excluding the camp-followers and workmen. They fled before 10,000 men, and Shir Khan gained a victory, whilst the Chaghatais were defeated, on this battle-field where not a man, either friend or foe, was wounded. Not a gun was fired, and the chariots were useless.

When the Chaghatais were defeated, the distance between their position and the Ganges might be nearly a parasang. All the amirs and braves fled for safety to the river, without a man of them having received a wound. The enemy pursued them, and the Chaghatais, having no time to throw off their armour and coats, plunged into the water. Many illustrious amirs were drowned, and each one remained, or went on, at his will. When we came out of the river, his Majesty, who at midday had a retinue of 17,000 in attendance upon his court, was mounted upon a horse which had been given him by Tardi

Beg, and had nothing on his head or feet. "Permanence is from God and dominion is from God." Out of a thousand retainers, eight persons came out of the river; the rest had perished in the water. The total loss may be estimated from this fact. When we reached Agra we made no tarry, but, broken and dispirited, in a state heart-rending to relate, we went on to Lahore.

—34—

HOW HUMAYUN MARRIED THE FUTURE MOTHER OF AKBAR.

[Gul-badan's *Memoirs.*
Trans. Mrs. A. S. Beveridge.]

Concerning Hamida-banu Begam, his Majesty asked, "Who is this?" They said, "The daughter of Mir Baba Dost". . . .

1541. In those days Hamida-banu Begam was often in the Mirza [Hindal]'s *mahall.* Another day when his Majesty came to see her Highness my mother, he remarked, "Mir Baba Dost is related to us. It is fitting that you should give me his daughter in marriage." Mirza Hindal kept on making objections, and said, " I look on this girl as a sister and child of my own. Your Majesty is a king. Heaven forbid that there should not be a proper alimony and that so a cause of annoyance should arise." His Majesty [who was then poor after his defeats by Shir Shah] got angry, and rose and went away. Then my mother wrote and sent a letter, saying, "The girl's mother has even before this been using persuasion. It is astonishing that you should go away in anger over a few words." He wrote in reply, "Your story is very welcome to me. Whatever persuasion you may use, by my head and my eyes, I will agree to it. As for what they have written about alimony, please Heaven, what they ask will be done. My waiting eye is upon the road". . . . On another day he came to my mother and said, "Send some one to call Hamida-banu Begam here." When she sent, the Begam did not come, but said, "If it is to pay my respects, I was exalted by paying my respects the other day. Why should I come again?. . . . To see Kings once is lawful; a second time is forbidden. I shall not come." . . . For forty days the Begam resisted and discussed and disagreed. At last her Highness my mother, Dil-dar Begam, advised her, saying, "After all, you will marry some one. Better than a King who is there?" The Begam said, "Oh yes, I shall marry some one; but he shall be a man whose collar my hand can touch, and not one whose skirt it does not reach." Then my mother gave her much advice. At last, after much discussion, at midday. . . . [September, 1541], his Majesty took the astrolabe into his own blessed hand, and having chosen a propitious hour, summoned Mir Abu-l-Baka and ordered him to make fast the marriage bond. He gave the Mir two lacs of ready money for the dower, and having stayed three days after the wedding in Patr, he set out and went by boat to Bhakkar. . . .

In 'Amarkot, in the early morning of Sunday, the 4th [5th] day of the revered Rajab,* 949 H. there was born his
15 Oct. Imperial Majesty, the world's refuge and conqueror,
1542. Jalal-ad-din Muhammad Akbar Ghazi. The moon was in Leo. It was of very good omen that the birth was in a fixed sign, and the astrologers said a child so born would be fortunate and long-lived.

* According to Jauhar, it was 14 Sha'ban (23 November).

— 35 —

HUMAYUN AT KABUL.

[Gul-badan's *Memoirs.*
Trans. Mrs. A. S. Beveridge.]

On his return from Badakhshan the Emperor spent a year and a half in Kabul and thus resolved to go to Balkh. He
1549. took up his quarters in the Heart-expanding Garden. . . . The Begams said to the Emperor over and over again, "Oh, how the *riwaj* [rhubarb] will be coming up." He replied, "When I join the army, I shall travel by the Koh-daman, so that you may come out and see the *riwaj* growing." It was at afternoon prayer-time that he rode out [of Kabul] to the garden. Kuli Beg's house, where the Begams were, was close by and overlooked it, and his Majesty pulled up as he passed, and all the Begams saw him, and rose and made the *kornish* [obeisance]. Directly they had made this salutation, he beckoned with his own blessed hand to say, "Come."

Fakhr-an-nisa mama and Afghani aghacha went on a little ahead. There was a stream in the lower part of the garden which Afghani aghacha could not cross, and she fell off her horse. For this reason there was an hour's delay. At last we set out with his Majesty. Mahchuchak Begam not knowing, her horse went up a little. His Majesty was very much annoyed about this. The garden was on a height and the walls were not yet made. Some vexation now showed itself in his blessed countenance, and he was pleased to say, "All of you go on and I will follow when I have taken some opium and got over my annoyance." He joined us when we had, as he ordered, gone on a little. The look of vexation was entirely laid aside and he came with a happy and beautiful look in his face. It was a moonlit night. We talked and told stories, and [several of us] sang softly, softly . . .

Everywhere in the Daman-Koh the *riwaj* had put up its leaves. We went to the skirts of the hills and when it was evening we walked about.

—36—

SHIR SHAH'S GOVERNMENT.

['Abbas Khan : *Ta'rikh-i-Shir-Shahi.*]

Shir Shah attended to every business concerning the administration of the kingdom and the revenues, great or small,
1545. in his own person. Nor did he permit his temporal affairs to be unmixed with devotion; day and night he was employed in both works. He had his attendants to wake him when two thirds of the night were passed, and after bathing he betook himself to prayer and supplication until the fourth watch. After that he heard the accounts of the various officers, and the ministers made their reports and recorded the orders of Shir Shah for the work to be done. When the morning had well broken he again performed his ablutions and with a great concourse went through the prescribed prayers. After that his chiefs and soldiers paid their respects, marshals announcing their names. About the first hour of day he performed the supererogatory prayer *Namaz-i-ishrak*. After this he asked the chiefs and soldiers as to assigning them *jagirs* [fiefs] before entering on a campaign, since none might ask for one during the war without punishment. He asked if there were any oppressed or ill-treated, that he might right them; for Shir Shah was adorned with the jewel of justice. He never favoured oppressors, though his near of kin, nor ever delayed punishing them. Then he mustered and paid his old troops and spoke to the recruits, and questioned the

Afghans in their own tongue. If one answered him well and drew a good bow at his order he rewarded him with better pay; for, said he, "I reckon the Afghan tongue as a friend." Then he inspected the treasure and gave audiences and received reports. When two hours and a half of the day were over, he breakfasted with his ulama, and then went on with business till midday.

Every year or second year he changed his amirs and sent new ones; for he said, "I have carefully examined and ascertained that there is no such income and profit in any office as in the government of a district. Therefore I send my good old loyal experienced servants to take charge of districts that they rather than others may receive the salaries and profits; and I change them after two years that others like them may also prosper." Shir Shah always kept about him 150,000 horsemen and 25,000 infantry, armed with matchlocks or bows, and on campaigns he had more, and kept garrisons wherever they were needed. After a time he would call in the troops which had enjoyed ease and comfort on their *jagirs*, and send away in turn the men who had toiled and endured in his victorious army.

He set up courts of justice in every place, and ever was busy in founding charities. For the easement of poor travellers he made a rest-house on every road at an interval of two *kos* [leagues], and one such road with rest-houses ran from the Panjab to Sunargaon in Bengal, and others from Agra to Burhanpur and to Chitor, and from Lahore to Multan. In each rest-house were separate lodgings for Hindus and Muslims, supplied with pots of water, beds, and food, and grain for the horses. In each rest-house two horses were kept for quick despatch of news. "If my life last long enough," he said, "I will build a fort in every sarkar, to be a refuge for the oppressed and a curb to the turbulent, and I make all the earthen rest-houses now of brick for the safety and protection of the highway." If a robbery occurred and the perpetrators not discovered, the 'amils and governors were instructed to arrest the headmen of the neighbouring villages and compel them to make it good. For it has been generally established that highway robberies occur only by the connivance of these headmen; but in the days of Shir Shah and Islam Shah these *mukaddams* protected their boundaries in the interests of travellers. It was a rule that the armies should do no injury to the people's cultivation.

— 37 —

AKBAR'S SIEGE OF CHITOR.

[Maulana Ahmad: *Ta'rikh-i-Alfi.*]

So the Emperor determined to attack Chitor, which is an exceedingly strong fortress. When he came near it, the rains

1567-8. were so heavy that for a time the fort was invisible, but as the weather cleared he got a view of the place. The fortress stands on a hill in the midst of a level plain which has no other hills, and the circuit of its base is six *kos* [15 miles] and the ground upon which the walls are built nearly three *kos*. Upon the hill top there is a spring, but the builders, not content with this, made great tanks of stone and mortar which get filled in the rains, so that the garrison never runs short of water. On the east and northerly sides the fort is faced with hard stone and the garrison feel safe about this part. Nor on the other sides, if guns and catapults should reach the fort, could they do much damage.

All the ground at the top was occupied, and the houses rose to several storeys. The battlements were numerously guarded and great stores of ammunition were in the fort.

Akbar carefully reconnoitred the place all round, and saw that it would not fall without a long siege. When the garrison noted the small force of only three or four thousand horsemen which he had brought, they shouted their scorn. But the batteries were distributed among the amirs, and every day some one arrived and went to his allotted battery ; so that the fort was soon invested. Day by day the besiegers brought their attack closer on every side, and many suffered martyrdom from the vigorous defenders. Trenches were dug and *sabats* [a kind of penthouse] constructed, and some five thousand builders, carpenters, masons, smiths, and sappers were collected from all parts. Two *sabats* were begun ; that opposite the royal quarters was so broad that two elephants and two horses could easily pass through it abreast, and so high that an elephant rider could carry his spear upright. The *sabats* were begun from the middle of the hill.

The defenders had never seen a *sabat* and were perplexed, but they tried to stop the work. Seven or eight thousand horsemen and numerous gunners attacked them, and thick as the hide-roofs of the shelters were, a hundred or more of the workmen fell daily, and their bodies were used instead of stones. They were not pressed, for the Emperor would not allow compulsion, but heaps of money were scattered. Soon a *sabat* reached and overlooked the walls, and on the top of it a seat was made whence Akbar could view the assaults of his men at his ease and take a part if he were so minded. Whilst the garrison were occupied with the *sabat*, the engineers made several mines under the walls, whilst the masons prised out with their crowbars any stones that blocked the line of the mine. Two bastions facing the royal quarters were thus undermined and the mines filled with gunpowder, whilst three or four hundred of the bravest men stood by ready to rush through the breach. Both mines were fired, and one of them sent a bastion flying into the air, its stones falling at a distance; a great breach was opened, and the storming party rushed in shouting their war-cry, only to be met by a strong force of the garrison; but whilst the struggle was at its height between these two in the other bastion, the second mine exploded and blew friend and foe together into the air, scattering their limbs in all directions. Stones of 50 and 100 *maunds* were hurled two or three *kos* off, and corpses were found for two *kos* round. Vast numbers of the garrison were killed, and the dust and smoke held back the Imperial army, under a shower of fragments, while the enemy bravely hid their losses.

The Emperor, seeing all this, redoubled his efforts, resolved to take this strongest of fortresses in Hindustan by storm, that no other fort should dare to resist him. He had the other *sabat* pushed forward and himself took his place on its roof, whence he shot every living thing that met his eye, whilst his men kept up a continual discharge from their bows
1568. and matchlocks. On the 5th Sha'ban 955 H. the assault was made. The walls had been breached in several places, and victory seemed to be at hand. Jai Mal, the commandant of the fortress, a valiant unbeliever, struggled all day in every part urging on his men. At the evening prayer he came in front of the royal battery where Akbar was firing his piece as often as a light flashed in the bastion. The ball struck Jai Mal in the forehead and killed him on the

spot. Their leader fallen, the garrison gave up hope. They burnt his body and then celebrated the Hindu rite of *jauhar* in their homes. *Jauhar* is this: when they are certain that escape is impossible, they gather together their wives and children and goods, heap firewood round them and set it alight; then when all these are burnt, they rush into the fight and meet their death. It is with them a great act of devotion.

The flames of the *jauhar* and the lull in the fighting showed the besiegers that the garrison was in extremities, and they began to enter the fort in parties. Some of the boldest of the garrison who had no families to burn, stood to their posts ready to sell their lives in defence. From the top of the *sabat* the Emperor viewed the combats, and ordered three elephants to be ridden into the town. One of them, Madkar, killed many of the enemy and though often wounded never turned tail; another, Jagna, was surrounded and killed with spears and swords. In the last watch of the night the besiegers forced their way into the fortress and fell to slaughter and pillage. At early dawn the Emperor rode in on an elephant, attended on foot by his nobles and chiefs. A general massacre was ordered. There were at least eight thousand fighting Rajputs in the fort. Some took their stand in the temple and fought to the last. In every street and lane and bazar there was desperate fighting. Now and again a band of Rajputs, throwing away hope of life, rushed from the temple and were despatched in detail. By mid-day some two thousand were slain. Those who escaped were made prisoners and their property confiscated.

—38—

AKBAR'S HUNTING.

[Nizam-ad-din : *Tabakat-i-Akbari.*]

At the beginning of the twelfth year of his reign [974-5 H.] which was near the Nauroz, his Majesty was pleased to order
1567. a kamarga [drive] hunt. For forty miles round Lahore the great amirs were to drive the game towards a large plain, some five *kos* from the city and about the same extent on every side, where the Emperor's tent was pitched; and thither some fifteen thousand deer, nilgaus, jackals, foxes, etc., were driven, and the amirs and khans drew the lines closer and narrowed the circle, while the Emperor hunted on horseback. After a few days' sport, he gave the attendants leave to shoot, so that every one got some game. Then the Emperor returned to the city, swimming his horse across the river; but two of his followers were drowned. During the hunt one of his favourite equerries, being drunk, wounded another attendant with an arrow, whereat the Emperor ordered Kalij Khan to strike off the equerry's head. But his sword broke harmlessly on the culprit's neck: so Akbar respited him but had him exposed to public derision.

There were many wild asses in this desert country [Nagor, Rajputana], and his Majesty, who had never hunted this ani-
1570. mal, heard one day that there were some near the camp. He at once mounted a fleet horse and, after riding four or five *kos*, came in sight of the herd. Dismounting and cautioning silence, he and four or five Biluchis who knew the country stalked the herd, which bolted in fright, after he had killed an ass with his first shot. His Majesty continued to stalk them, till he had dropped sixteen. He covered seventeen *kos* whilst hunting that day, and returned to camp where the asses' flesh was distributed among the courtiers.

— 39 —

AT THE FERRY OF MANIKPUR.

[Nizam-ad-din : *Tabakat-i-Akbari.*]

There the Emperor Akbar crossed the [swollen] river on an elephant, and a thousand to fifteen hundred men swam
1568. along with him. On Sunday, 1st Zu-l-Hijja, 974 H.
he made his dispositions for action: he himself took command of the centre; Asaf Khan was on the right, Majnun Khan and other amirs on the left. The enemy drew out their forces and attacked the Emperor's advanced guard, but were repulsed and driven back upon the lines of 'Ali Kuli Khan, whereat Bahadur Khan charged the advanced guard and in turn drove it back upon Majnun's troops. Bahadur got between the two, his horse being wounded and unmanageable, and was taken prisoner. The fight waxing hot, Akbar descended from his elephant, Balsundar, and mounted a horse, and ordered the elephants to be driven against 'Ali Kuli Khan's lines. One of them, called Hiranand, butted an enemy elephant, Diyana, so that he fell upon the spot. 'Ali Kuli Khan was wounded by an arrow, and his horse too, and he was thrown. An elephant, Narsing, was about to crush him, when he called to the driver "I am a great man: take me alive to the Emperor and he will reward you"; but the man took no notice and drove the elephant over him and trampled him to death. Bahadur Khan was brought to the Emperor, and, at the instance of the amirs, executed. Presently 'Ali Kuli's head was brought in. The Emperor dismounted and gave thanks for this victory. The battle was fought near the village of Mankarwal.

—40—

THE FORTRESS OF SURAT.

[Nizam-ad-din: *Tabakat-i-Akbari.*]

The fortress of Surat is small but exceedingly strong, secure, and peculiar, and was built, it is said, in 947 H. by Khudawand Khan, an officer of Sultan Mahmud of Gujarat, to repel the attacks of the Europeans; for before it was built they did much mischief to the Muslims. Whilst he was building it, they several times sent their ships against it but failed to take it. To make it more safe, Khudawand's architect contrived, on the two sides of the fort exposed to land attack, ditches, built of stone, chunam, and burnt brick, twenty yards wide, filled with water, reaching to the sea. The four walls are fifteen yards thick and twenty high, and each stone is clamped to the next with iron, and with molten lead poured into the interstices. The formidable battlements and embrasures are of stone, and on the top is a *chaukandi* [belvedere], which Europeans think is an invention of the Portuguese. When they were unable by force to stop the fort being built, the Europeans offered large sums to Khudawand to desist, but he
1573. persisted. After it was taken in 980 the Emperor noticed some large mortars, which were called Sulaimani after the Sultan of Turkey, who had sent them by sea during his invasion of Gujarat. The Turks on their retreat left these guns on the sea shore, and Khudawand transferred them to the new fort of Surat. The Emperor had them removed to Agra. One gun left behind by the Turks had been brought into the fort of Junagarh by its ruler.

—41—

REVENUE REFORMS.

[Badauni: *Ta'rikh.*]

In this year 982 an order was promulgated for improving the cultivation of the country and the condition of the rayats.

1575. All the parganas were to be measured and every space of land which under cultivation would produce a kror of tankas was to be divided off and placed under an officer called the *krori*, selected for his trustworthiness, whether known or unknown to the revenue clerks and treasurers, so that in three years all the uncultivated land might be brought into cultivation and the public treasury replenished. Regulations were circulated but were not properly observed. A large part of the land was laid waste by the rapacity of the kroris, the rayats' wives and children were sold and scattered, and all was confusion. But the kroris were brought to account by Raja Todar Mal, and many a good man died from severe beatings and the torture of rack and pincers.

—42—

THE HALL OF DIVINE WORSHIP.

[Nizam-ad-din: *Tabakat-i-Akbari.*]

From early youth the Emperor delighted in the society of learned and gifted men and the meetings of men of genius,

1575. and treated them with the utmost respect. He listened to their discussions of nice points of science, ancient and modern history, religions and sects, etc., and he profited by what he heard. On his return from Ajmir at the close of 982 H., in the 20th year of his reign, he ordered skilful architects and builders to erect in the royal gardens [at Fathpur Sikri] a home for holy men where none should enter but distinguished sayyids, ulama, and shaikhs. They planned a building with four halls, [transepts, *iwans*], and when it was finished the Emperor went there on Fridays and holy nights and would sit till dawn in the society of men of intellect. The sayyids were allotted the west transept, the ulama the south, and the shaikhs and mystics had the south transept, without confusion or mingling. In the east portion sat the nobles and court officials. His Majesty graced each section with his presence and enriched the assembly by his bounty; for they used to elect from among themselves those most worthy to be presented to him, and he would give them handfuls of money; whilst those who had not the good luck to be so favoured used to sit down in rows before this *'Ibadat Khana* [Hall of Divine Worship] on Fridays and receive largesse from his hands, till he was tired—these levees lasting often beyond noon—and left this distribution to his attendants.

[Badauni: *Ta'rikh.*]

In 983 the Hall of Divine Worship was finished. The reason it was built was this: In recent years the Emperor had won a series of victories, till no enemy was left. He had taken a liking for the society of ascetics, spent much time in discussing the word of God and the Prophet's sayings, and showed an interest in Sufism, science and philosophy. He passed whole nights meditating upon God and the modes of addressing him. Reverence for the great Giver filled his heart, and in gratitude he would sit many a morning alone in prayer and mortification upon the stone bench of an old cell in a lonely spot near the palace. Thus meditating he gathered the bliss of the first hours of dawn.

His Majesty used often to go to the 'Ibadat Khana and converse with the ulama and shaikhs, especially on Sabbath evenings, and would sometimes pass the whole night there. The discussions always turned upon religion, upon its principles, and its divarications. The learned doctors used to exercise the sword of their tongues upon each other and showed great pugnacity and animosity, till each sect took to calling the rest infidels and perverts. Innovators and schismatics artfully started their doubts and sophistries, making right appear wrong, and wrong right. And so his Majesty, who had an excellent understanding and sought after the truth but was surrounded by low irreligious persons, was plunged into scepticism. Doubt was piled upon doubt, and the object of his search was lost. The ramparts of the law and the true faith were broken down, and in the course of five or six years not one trace of Islam was left in him.

Learned men from every country and professors of various religions came to his Court and were admitted to converse with him. Night and day people did nothing but inquire and investigate. He collected the opinions of everyone, especially of non-Muslims, keeping what he approved and rejecting what ran counter to his wishes. From early childhood he had passed through the most diverse phases of religious practices and beliefs and collected with a peculiar talent in selection all that books can teach, and thus there gradually grew in his mind the conviction that there were sensible men in all religions and austere thinkers and men with miraculous gifts in all nations. If some truth was thus found everywhere, why should truth be restricted to one religion or to a comparatively new creed like Islam, scarcely a thousand years old?

Moreover Samanis [ascetics] and Brahmans frequently collogued with him in private, and these, being above all others learned in ethics and natural and theological sciences, in prognostication and spiritual power and perfection, brought such proofs in reason and evidence and pressed their doctrines so relentlessly, skilfully representing as self-evident things which require reasoning, that no man's doubts could raise an echo in his Majesty, though mountains might crumble to dust and the heavens gape open. He listened to every abuse which the courtiers heaped on our glorious and pure faith of Islam, so easy to follow, and showed his satisfaction at the way they received his own original religion.

In 986 the missionaries of Europe who are called Padres and whose chief pontiff, called Papa, promulgates his conclusions for the use of his people and issues mandates that kings dare not disobey, brought their Gospel to his Majesty's notice, showed their proofs of the Trinity, and spread the knowledge of the religion of Jesus. The King ordered Prince Murad to learn a few lessons from the Gospel and to treat it with all respect, and Shaikh Abu-l-Fazl was directed to translate it. Instead of the prologue "Bismillah" the formula "O thou whose names are Jesus and Christ" was enjoined.

The accursed Birbal tried to persuade the King that since the sun gives light to all, ripens all grain and fruits and products of the earth and supports man's life, it ought to be worshipped, and the face should be turned towards its rising, not its setting, etc. Several wise men at Court confirmed what he said, adding that the sun was a friend to Kings who fixed periods and eras according to its motions. This was the cause of the worship paid to the sun [by Akbar] and his adopting Nauroz [the Vernal Equinox] as his accession festival. He suited his clothes in colour to the regent planet of the day and muttered Hindu spells to influence the sun in his favour. He forbade the slaughter of cows and the eating of their flesh. From early youth, in compliment to his Rajput wives, he had burnt the *hom*; but on the New Year festival of the 25th year of his reign he prostrated himself in public before the sun and before the fire, and in the evening the whole court had to rise respectfully when the lamps and candles were lighted. On the feast of the eighth day after the sun's entering Virgo he came forth to the public audience chamber with his forehead marked like a Hindu and with jewelled strings tied by Brahmans on his wrist. In defiance and contempt of the true faith, every precept enjoined by other religions he adopted as obvious and decisive. Those of Islam he esteemed follies. These sentiments had long been growing in his mind and ripened gradually to firm conviction.

[Abu-l-Fazl: *Akbar-nama.*]

When the capital [Fathpur Sikri] was illumined by the return of the Imperial presence, the house of wisdom shone resplendent on Friday nights with the light of the holy mind. On the 20th Mihr [3 Oct. 1578], in that place of meeting, the lamp was kindled to brighten the solitude of seclusion in the banquet of society, and the merits of the philosophers of the colleges and cells were put to the test of the touchstone. Sufis, doctors, orators, lawyers, Sunnis, Shi'is, Brahmans, ascetics, Jains, Charbaks, Christians, Jews, Sabians, Zoroastrians, learned men of every belief, were gathered together in the royal assembly and were filled with delight, beholding the world-lord in the lofty pulpit and the adornment of the abode of impartiality. Each fearlessly brought forward his assertions and arguments, and the disputations and contentions were long and heated .... One night the Hall of Worship was brightened by the presence of Padre Rodolpho [Acquaviva], unrivalled among Christian doctors for intellect and wisdom. Several carping and bigoted men attacked him, and this afforded an opportunity for a display of the calm judgment and justice of the assembly. These men brought forward the old received assertions and did not attempt to arrive at the truth by reasoning. Their statements were torn to pieces and they were nearly put to shame; and then they began to attack the contradictions in the Gospel, but they could not silence their opponent by proving their assertions. With perfect calmness and earnest conviction, the Padre replied to their arguments, and then said, "If these men have such an opinion of our Book, and if they believe the Koran to be the true word of God, then let a fire be lighted and let us with the Gospel in our hand, and the 'ulama with their holy Book in theirs, walk into that testing-place of truth, and the right will be manifest." The black-hearted mean-spirited disputants shrank from this proposal, and answered only with angry words.

This cowardice and effrontery greatly annoyed the impartial mind of the Emperor, and with great discrimination and enlightenment he said, "Men fancy that outward profession and the mere letter of Islam, without a heartfelt conviction, can profit them. I have forced many Hindus, by fear of my power, to adopt the religion of my ancestors; but now that my mind has been enlightened by the beams of truth, I have become convinced that in this distressful place of contrarieties, where the dark clouds of conceit and the mist of self-opinion have gathered round you, not a step can be made in advance without the torch of proof. That belief only can be beneficial which we select with clear judgement. To repeat the words of the Creed, to perform circumcision, or to lie prostrate on the ground from dread of kingly power, is not seeking God.

Obedience is not in prostration on the dust ;
Practise truth, for sincerity is not borne upon the brow."

—43—

THE TEN YEARS' SETTLEMENT.

[Abu-l-Fazl: *Aïn-i-Akbari.*]

From the beginning of this immortal reign persons of intelligence and void of rapacity, together with zealous men of experience, have been annually engaged in noting the current prices and reporting them to his Majesty, and taking the gross produce and estimating its value they determined the rates of collection: but this mode was attended with considerable inconvenience. The total revenue was taken at an estimation: and the assignments were increased at the caprice of the moment; variations were contingent on the extent of corruption and self-interest. Under Muzaffar Khan and Raja Todar Mal, in the 15th year of the reign, a redistribution of the imperial assessment was made; although this was somewhat less than the preceding one, yet there was a wide discrepancy between the estimate and the receipts. As the empire increased in extent it became more difficult to ascertain current prices, and delay caused much inconvenience.

The husbandman complained of excessive exactions, and the landholder was aggrieved by the revenue balances. His Majesty devised a remedy for these evils and fixed
1570-1580. a settlement for ten years: from the beginning of the 15th year of the Divine Era to the 24th, an aggregate of the rates of collection was computed and a tenth of this total was fixed as the annual assessment; but from the 20th to the 24th year the collections were accurately determined, and the five earlier ones accepted on the authority of persons of probity. The best crops were taken into account in each year, and the year of the most abundant harvest accepted.

— 44 —

THE ILAHI ERA.

[Abu-l-Fazl: *Aïn-i-Akbari.*]

His Majesty had long desired to introduce a new computation of years and months throughout the fair regions of Hindustan in order that perplexity might give place to easiness. He was likewise averse to the era of the Hijra, which was of ominous signification; but because of the number of short-sighted ignorant men who believe the currency of the era to be inseparable from religion, he did not carry out
1584. his design (of suppressing it). In 992 of the novi-lunar year, the lamp of knowledge received another light from the flame of his sublime intelligence and its full blaze shone upon mankind. The imperial design was accomplished. Amir Fath-Allah Shirazi, taking as his basis the Gurgani Canon, began the era with the accession of his Imperial Majesty. The years and months are natural solar without intercalation and the Persian names of the months and days have been left unaltered. The days of the month are from 29 to 32.

— 45 —

AKBAR ON PAINTING.

[Abu-l-Fazl: *Aïn-i-Akbari.*]

I have to notice that the observing of the figures of objects and the making a likeness of them, which are often looked upon as an idle occupation, are for a well-regulated mind a source of wisdom and an antidote against the poison of ignorance. Bigoted followers of the letter of the law are hostile to the art of painting; but their eyes now see the truth. One day in a private party of friends his Majesty, who had conferred on several the pleasure of drawing near him, remarked, "There are many that hate painting, but such men I dislike. It appears to me as if a painter had quite peculiar means of recognizing God; for a painter, in sketching anything that has life, and in devising its limbs one after the other, must come to feel that he cannot confer personality upon his work, and is thus forced to think of God, the Giver of life, and will thus increase in knowledge."

— 46 —

AKBAR'S HABITS.

[Abu-l-Fazl: *Aïn-i-Akbari.*]

Every afternoon, one *ghari* [24 minutes] before sunset, his Majesty, if on horseback, alights, or if sleeping is awakened.
1596-7. He then lays aside the splendour of royalty and brings his outer looks into harmony with his heart. And when the sun sets, the attendants light twelve white candles on twelve gold and silver candlesticks and bring them before his Majesty, when a singer of sweet

melodies, candle in hand, sings delightful airs to the praise of God, beginning and ending with a prayer for the continuance of this auspicious reign.

To make the royal camp conspicuous to those who come from afar, his Majesty has set up in front of the Durbar a forty yards pole, stayed by sixteen ropes, and on the top is a large lantern, called the "Skylamp" [Akasdiah], the gleam of which is seen from a great way off and guides soldiers to the camp and to their tents.

If his Majesty did not possess so lofty a mind, so comprehensive an understanding, so universal a kindness, he would have chosen the path of solitude and given up sleep and food altogether: and even now, when he has taken upon himself the temporal and spiritual leadership of the people, the question "What dinner has been prepared to-day?" never passes over his tongue. In the course of twenty-four hours his Majesty eats but once and leaves off before he is fully satisfied; nor is there any fixed time for this meal, but the servants always have things so far ready that an hour after the order is given a hundred dishes are served up.

The food for the women of the harim begins to come from the kitchen in the morning and goes on till night. Trusty experienced people are set over the kitchen department; their chief is advised by the Prime Minister himself, to whom his Majesty has especially intrusted this important department, as well as affairs of state. Cooks from all countries prepare a great variety of dishes of all kinds of grains, greens, meats; also oily, sweet, and spicy dishes. The victuals are served up in dishes of gold and silver, stone and earthenware. During the cooking and taking out, an awning is spread and onlookers are kept away; the cooks tuck up their sleeves and the hems of their garments and hold their hands before their mouths and noses while the food is being taken out; the cook and manciple taste it, and then the Head Manciple (Mir Bakawal) tastes it, and it is put into the dishes. The gold and silver dishes are tied up in red cloths and the copper and china in white, and they are sealed by the Head Manciple, who writes the contents on each dish, whilst the pantry clerk writes a list, sealed by the Head Manciple, of all the vessels and dishes which are sent in, so that none of them may be changed. After it is carried in by the cooks, the servants of the palace again taste the food, spread the table-cloth on the ground, and arrange the dishes; and when after some time his Majesty begins his dinner, the table servants sit opposite to wait on him; first the share of the poor [fakirs] is set aside, and then his Majesty begins with milk or curds. After dinner, he falls in prayer. The Head Manciple is always in attendance.

His Majesty cares very little for meat; if he had not the burden of the world on his shoulders he would at once totally abstain from it; and now it is his intention to quit it by degrees, conforming, however, a little to the spirit of the age.

His Majesty is very fond of perfumes and encourages this department from religious motives. The court-hall is continually scented with ambergris, aloes-wood, and compounds made from ancient recipes or invented by himself; and incense is daily burnt in gold and silver censers, whilst sweet-smelling flowers are used in abundance.

— 47 —

SATI.

[Abu-l-Fazl: *Akbar-nama.*]

It is the custom in Hindustan for a widow willingly and cheerfully to cast herself into the flames of her husband's pyre; but sometimes if from wickedness and love of life she refrain from doing this, her husband's relations light the flame, whether she be willing or unwilling; thinking to preserve the honour of the family. But since the rule of his glorious Majesty, inspectors had been set in every city and district, who were to watch carefully and discriminate between these two cases, and prevent any woman being forcibly burnt. [When Jai Mal died of sunstroke] near Causa, his widow, the daughter of Mota Raja, had not the courage to burn herself, but her son Udai Singh with his bigoted friends resolved upon the sacrifice. It was high dawn when the news came to the Emperor's harim, and fearing delay if he sent messengers [to stop the act], he mounted a swift horse and rode to the place. In a short time the prudent prince made use of justice, graciousness, and courage, and brought things into tranquillity.

— 48 —

FIRST TRIAL OF TOBACCO.

[Asad Beg: *Wikaya.*]

In Bijapur I had found some tobacco. Never having seen the like in India, I brought some with me and prepared a
1604. handsome pipe of jewel work. The stem, the finest to be procured in Achin, was three cubits in length, beautifully dried and coloured, both ends being adorned with jewels and enamel. I happened to come across a very handsome mouthpiece of Yemen cornelian: oval-shaped, which I set to the stem: the whole was very handsome. There was also a golden burner for lighting it. 'Adil Khan had given me a betel bag of very superior workmanship; this I filled with fine tobacco, such that if one leaf be lit the whole will continue burning. I arranged all elegantly on a silver tray.

His Majesty was enjoying himself after receiving my presents and asking me how I had collected so many strange things in so short a time, when his eye fell upon the tray with the pipe and its appurtenances; he expressed great surprise and examined the tobacco which was made up in pipefuls; he inquired what it was and where I had got it. The Nawab Khan-i-A'zam replied, "This is tobacco, which is well-known in Mecca and Medina, and this doctor has brought it as a medicine for your Majesty." Akbar looked at it, and ordered me to prepare and give him a pipeful. He began to smoke it, when his physician approached and forbade his doing so. But his Majesty was graciously pleased to say he must smoke a little to gratify me, and taking the mouthpiece into his sacred mouth drew two or three breaths. The physician was in great anxiety and would not let him do more. He took the pipe from his mouth and bade the Khan-i-A'zam try it, who took two or three puffs. He then sent for his druggist, and asked what were its peculiar qualities. He replied that there was no mention of it in his books; but that it was a new invention, and the stems were imported from China, and European doctors had written much in its praise. The first physician said, "In fact, this is an untried medicine, about which the doctors have written nothing. How can we describe to your Majesty the qualities of such unknown things? It is not fitting that your Majesty should try it." I answered, "The Europeans are not so foolish as not to know all about it; there are wise men among them who seldom err or make mistakes. How can you, before you have tried a thing and found out its qualities, pass a judgement on it that can be depended on? Things must be judged according to their merits." The physician replied, "We do not want to follow the Europeans and adopt a custom which is not sanctioned by our own wise men." I said, "It is a strange thing, for every custom in the world has been new at one time or another; from the days of Adam till now, they have gradually been invented. When a new thing is introduced among the people and becomes well known in the world, everybody adopts it." The Emperor heard me reason with the physician with astonishment and was much pleased. He gave me his blessing, and said to Khan-i-A'zam, "Did you hear how wisely Asad spoke? Truly, we must not reject a thing that has been adopted by the wise men of other nations, merely because we cannot find it in our books; or how shall we progress?" The physician was going to say more, but his Majesty stopped him and called for a priest. The priest ascribed many good qualities to tobacco, but no one could persuade the physician; nevertheless he was a good physician.

As I had brought a large supply of tobacco and pipes, I sent some to several of the nobles, whilst others sent to ask for it; indeed, all, without exception, wanted some and the practice of smoking was introduced. After that, the merchants began selling it, so the custom spread rapidly. His Majesty, however, did not adopt it.

—49—

CHARACTER OF AKBAR.

[Jahangir's *Memoirs*.
Trans. A. Rogers and H. Beveridge.]

My father always associated with the learned of every creed and religion: especially the Pundits and the learned of India, and although he was illiterate, so much became clear to him through constant intercourse with the learned and wise, in his conversations with them, that no one knew him to be illiterate, and he was so well acquainted with the niceties of verse and prose compositions, that his deficiency was not thought of.

In his august personal appearance he was of middle height, but inclining to be tall; he was of the hue of wheat; his eyes and eyebrows were black, and his complexion rather dark than fair; he was lion-bodied, with a broad chest, and his hands and arms long. On the left side of his nose he had a fleshy mole, very agreeable in appearance, of the size of half a pea. Those skilled in the science of physiognomy considered this mole a sign of great prosperity and exceeding good fortune. His august voice was very loud, and in speaking and explaining had a peculiar richness. In his actions and movements he was not like the people of the world, and the glory of God manifested itself in him.

Notwithstanding his kingship, his treasures and his buried wealth past computation, his fighting elephants and Arab horses, he never by a hair's breath placed his foot beyond the base of humility before the throne of God, and never for one moment forgot Him. He associated with the good of every race and creed and persuasion, and was gracious to all in accordance with their condition and understanding. He passed his nights in wakefulness, and slept little in the day; the length of his sleep during a whole night and day was not more than a watch and a half. He counted his wakefulness at night as so much added to his life.

His courage and boldness were such that he could mount raging rutting elephants and subdue to obedience murderous elephants which would not allow their own females near them. Of the austerities practised by my revered father one was the not eating the flesh of animals. During three months of the year he ate meat, and for the remaining nine contented himself with Sufi food and was in no way pleased with the slaughter of animals. On many days and in many months this was forbidden to the people.

—50—

THE TWELVE ORDINANCES OF JAHANGIR.

[Jahangir's *Memoirs.*
Trans. Rogers and Beveridge.]

After my accession, the first order that I gave was for the hanging up of the Chain of Justice, so that if those engaged
1605. in the administration of justice should delay or practise hypocrisy the oppressed might come to this chain and shake it to attract [my] attention.

I also gave twelve Ordinances to be observed as Rules of Conduct in all my dominions:—

1. Forbidding the levy of cesses and tolls and other burdens which the *jagirdars* (landholders) of every province and district had imposed for their own profit.

2. Rest-houses, mosques, and wells to be built by the *jagirdars* on lonely roads where robberies take place, to stimulate a resident population there.

3. Bales of merchants not to be opened on the road without their leave.

4. The property of the deceased, whether Muslim or unbeliever, to go to his heirs without interference; if no heirs, guardians to preserve and administer the property for the public good.

5. Wine, spirits, or intoxicating drugs not to be made or sold. I myself drank wine from the age of 18 till now when

I am 38, and have persisted in it. When I first took a liking to drinking I sometimes took as much as twenty cups of double-distilled spirit; when by degrees it acquired a great influence over me I endeavoured to lessen the quantity, and in the period of seven years I have brought myself from fifteen cups to five or six. Now I drink only to digest my food.

6. No person's house shall be seized.

7. No one's nose or ears shall be cut off. I vowed by the throne of God that I would not thus mutilate anybody.

8. Officials and *jagirdars* shall not take the rayats' lands by force and cultivate them on their own account.

9. A government collector or a *jagirdar* shall not without permission intermarry with the people of the *pargana* where he resides.

10. Hospitals shall be founded and physicians appointed to them in the great cities, to be paid out of the State revenue.

11. In accordance with the regulations of my revered father, animals shall not be slaughtered from my birthday each year for a number of days equal to my age; nor on Thursday, my accession day, or Sunday, my father's birthday. He held this day in great reverence on this account and because it was dedicated to the sun and also was the first day of the Creation.

12. The offices and *jagirs* of my father's servants are confirmed. Later the *mansabs* [commands or ranks] were increased by not less than 20 per cent. to 300 or 400 per cent. I increased the allowances of all the veiled ladies of my father's harim from 20 to 100 per cent. By a stroke of the pen I confirmed the mensal lands of the holders of charities, who form the army of prayer, according to their charters. I released all criminals who had been long confined in the forts and prisons.

—51—

MURDER OF ABU-L-FAZL.

[Jahangir's *Memoirs.*]

I promoted Raja Bir Singh Deo, a Bandela Rajput, who had obtained my favour, and who excels his equals and relations in valour, personal goodness, and simple-heartedness, to the rank of [a commander of] 3000. The reason for his advancement and for the regard shown to him was that near the end of my revered father's time Shaikh Abu-l-Fazl, who excelled the Shaikhzadas of Hindustan in wisdom and learning, had adorned himself outwardly with the jewel of sincerity and sold it to my father [Akbar] at a heavy price. He had been summoned from the Deccan, and, since his feelings toward me were not honest, he both publicly and privately spoke against me. At this period, when, through strife-exciting intriguers, the august feelings of my royal father were entirely embittered against me, it was certain that if the Shaikh obtained the honour of waiting upon him, it would be the cause of more confusion and preclude me from the favour of union with my father. It became necessary to prevent Abu-l-Fazl from coming to Court. As Bir Singh Deo's country was exactly on his route, and he was then a rebel, I sent him a message that if he would stop that sedition-monger and kill him he would receive every kindness from me. By God's grace, when Shaikh Abu-l-Fazl was passing through Bir Singh Deo's country, the Raja blocked his road, and after a little contest scattered his men
1602. and killed him. He sent his head to me at Allahabad. Though this event was a cause of anger in the mind of the late King, in the end it enabled me to proceed without disturbance of mind to kiss the threshold of my father's palace, and by degrees the resentment of the king was cleared away.

—52—

WEIGHING THE EMPEROR.

[Jahangir's *Memoirs.*]

On Wednesday, 9 Jumada-l-awwal, 21 Shahriwar, after three watches and four *gharis*, the feast of my solar weighing, which is the commencement of the 38th year of my
1606. age, took place. According to custom, they got ready the weighing apparatus and the scales in the house of [my mother] Maryam-zamani. At the moment, appointed blessings were invoked, and I sate in the scales. Each suspending rope was held by an elderly person who offered up prayers. The first time the weight in gold came to three Hindustani maunds and ten sirs [140 lbs.]. After this I was weighed against several metals, perfumes and essences, up to twelve weighings. Twice a year I weigh myself against gold and silver and other metals, and against all sorts of silks and cloths and various grains, etc., once at the beginning of the solar year and once at that of the lunar. The weight of the money of the two weighings I hand over to the different treasurers for fakirs and those in want.

—53—

PRINCE KHUSRAU'S CAPTURE AFTER REBELLION.

[Jahangir's *Memoirs.*]

On Thursday, Muharram 3rd, 1015, in Mirza Kamran's garden, they brought Khusrau before me with his hand tied

and chains on his legs. They made Husain Beg stand on his right hand and 'Abd-ar-Rahim on his left. Khusrau
1606. stood weeping and trembling between them. Husain Beg, in the idea that it might profit him, began to speak wildly. I did not allow him to go on talking, but handed over Khusrau in chains, and ordered these two villains to be put in the skins of an ox and an ass, and mounted on asses with their faces to the tail, be thus taken round the city. As the ox-hide dried more quickly than the ass's, Husain Beg remained alive for four watches and died from suffocation. 'Abd-ar-Rahim, who was in the ass's skin, and to whom they gave some refreshment from outside, survived.

—54—

JAHANGIR'S CUSTOM.

[Capt. William Hawkins : *Relations.*]

His custom is in every year to be out two months on hunting. If coming forth of his palace he get up on a horse, it is a sign that he goeth for the wars; but if he get
1609. upon an elephant or palanquin, it will be a hunting voyage. Myself, in the time I was one of his courtiers, have seen many cruel deeds done by him. Five times a week he commandeth his brave elephants to fight before him; and in the time of their fighting, either coming or going out, many times men are killed or dangerously hurt by these elephants. But if any be grievously hurt (which might very well escape) yet nevertheless that man is cast into the river, himself commanding it, saying, dispatch him, for as long as he liveth he will do nothing but curse me and therefore it

is better that he die presently. I have seen many in this kind. Again he delighteth to see men executed himself and torn in pieces with elephants.

Now here I mean to speak a little of his manners and customs in the Court. First in the morning about the break of day he is at his beads with his face turned to the westward. The manner of his praying when he is in Agra is in a private fair room, upon a goodly set stone, having only a Persian lamb-skin under him. At the upper end of this stone the pictures of our Lady and Christ are placed, graven in stone; so he turneth over his beads and saith 3200 words, according to the number of his beads, and then his prayer is ended. After he hath done, he showeth himself to the people, receiving their salams or good-morrows, unto whom multitudes resort every morning for this purpose. This done, he sleepeth two hours more, and then dineth, and passeth his time with his women; and at noon he showeth himself to the people again, sitting till three of the clock, viewing and seeing his pastimes and sports made by men and fighting of many sorts of beasts, every day sundry kinds of pastimes.

Then at three of the clock all the nobles in general, that be in Agra and are well, resort unto the Court, the King coming forth in open audience, sitting in his seat royal, and every man standing in his degree before him, his chiefest sort of nobles standing within a red rail, and the rest without. They are all placed by his lieutenant-general. This red rail is three steps higher than the place where the rest stand; and within this red rail I was placed, amongst the chiefest of them all. The rest are placed by officers, and they likewise be within another very spacious place railed; and without that rail stand all sorts of horsemen and soldiers that belong unto his captains and all other comers. At these rails there are many doors kept by many porters, who have white rods to keep men in order. In the midst of the place, right before the King, standeth one of his sheriffs, together with the master hangman, who is accompanied by forty hangmen, wearing on their heads a certain quilted cap different from all others, with a hatchet on their shoulders; and others with all sorts of whips, being there ready to do what the King commandeth. The King heareth all causes in this place and stayeth some two hours every day.

Then he departeth towards his private place of prayer; his prayer being ended, four or five sorts of very well dressed and roasted meats are brought him, of which as he pleaseth he eateth a bit to stay his stomach, drinking once of his strong drink. Then he cometh forth into a private room, where none can come but such as himself nominateth (for two years I was one of his attendants there). In this place he drinketh other three cupfuls, which is the portion that the physicians allot him. This done, he eateth opium, and then he ariseth, and being in the height of his drink, he layeth him down to sleep, every man departing to his own home. And after he hath slept two hours they awake him and bring his supper to him; at which time he is not able to feed himself; but it is thrust into his mouth by others; and this is about one of the clock; and then he sleepeth the rest of the night.

—55—

RULES FOR OFFICERS.

[Jahangir's *Memoirs.*]

Having again heard that the amirs on the borders interfere with authority in matters that do not concern them, and do

not obey rules and regulations, I commanded that the Bakh-
1612. shis should circulate orders that hereafter they
should not interfere in such things, which are the
private affairs of Kings.

The first thing is that they should not sit in the *jharokha* [display window], nor trouble their officers and captains of the auxiliaries with keeping guard or saluting them, and should not have elephant fights, and should not inflict the penalty of blinding nor cut off noses and ears, and should not force Islam on anyone, and not confer titles on their servants nor order the royal servants to perform *kornish* [obeisance] and should not force singers to remain on duty in the manner customary in durbars, and should not beat drums when they go out, and when they give a horse or elephant to anyone, they should not put reins or elephants' goads on their backs and make them do obeisance. In a procession they should not take the royal attendants with them on foot in their retinue. If they write to them, they are not to put a seal to it.

—56—

JAHANGIR AS A SPORTSMAN.

[Jahangir's *Memoirs.*]

Before this I had given leave to Zafar Khan to go to Baba Hasan Abdal to collect game together for sport. He had
1607. made a *shakhband* [ring]. Twenty-seven red deer
and sixty-eight white ones came into it. I myself struck with arrows 29 antelope, and Parwiz and Khurram also killed some others with arrows. Afterwards orders were given to the servants and courtiers to shoot. Khan Jahan was the best shot, and in every case of his striking an antelope the arrow penetrated through and through. Again on

the 14th of Rajab, Zafar Khan arranged a *kamarga* [drive] at Rawalpindi. I struck with an arrow a red deer at a long distance and was highly delighted at his falling down. Thirty-four red deer and thirty-five blacktailed antelope and two pigs were also killed. On the 21st another drive had been arranged within three leagues [*kos*] of the fort of Rohtas by the efforts and exertions of Hilal Khan. I had taken with me to this hunt those who were screened by the curtain of honour [zenana]. The hunt was a good one and came off with great *éclat*. Two hundred red and white antelope were killed. On the 24th another hunt took place in the neighbourhood of Rohtas. In this hunt also my sisters and the other ladies were with me, and nearly 100 red deer were killed. It was told me that Shams Khan, who was in that neighbourhood, notwithstanding his great age, took much delight in hunting, such that young men had not so much enjoyment in it. When I heard that he was well-disposed towards fakirs and dervishes I went to his house, and his disposition and manners pleased me. I bestowed on him 2000 rupees, and the same sum on his wives and children, with five other villages with large receipts by way of livelihood for them, that they might pass their days in comfort and contentment.

—57—

HUNTING SCORE.

[Jahangir's *Memoirs.*]

It occurred to me that I might make up the account of my game from the commencement of my years of discretion up to the present time. I accordingly gave orders to

1617. the newswriters and hunt accountants, etc. It was shown that from the commencement of my 12th year, which was in 988 [1580] up to the end of this year, which is the 11th after my accession and my 50th lunar year, 28,532 head of game had been taken in my presence. Of these, 17,167 animals I killed myself with my gun and otherwise, viz. quadrupeds, 3,203; viz. tigers, 86; bears, cheetahs, foxes, otters, and hyænas, 9; blue bulls [nilgao], 889; *mhaka* [markhor?], an antelope equal in size to a blue bull, 35; of antelope, male and female, *chikara, chital*, mountain goats, etc., 1670; rams and red deer, 215; wolves, 64; wild buffaloes, 36; pigs, 90; *rang* [ibex], 26; mountain sheep, 22; *arqhali*, 32; wild asses, 6; hares, 23. Birds, 13,964; viz. pigeons, 10,348; *lagar jhagar* [a species of hawk], 3; eagles, 2; kites, 23; owls [*chughd*], 39; *kantan*, 12; mice-eaters [kites], 5; sparrows, 41; doves, 25; owls [*bum*], 30; ducks, geese, cranes, etc., 150; crows, 3,276. Aquatic animals, 10 crocodiles.

—58—

NUR-JAHAN'S FIRST TIGERS.

[Jahangir's *Memoirs*.]

On the 7th Urdibihisht, as the huntsmen had marked down four tigers, when two watches and three gharis had passed, I
1617. went out to hunt them with my ladies. When the tigers came in sight, Nur-Jahan submitted that if I would order her she herself would kill the tigers with her gun I said "Let it be so." She shot two tigers with one shot each and knocked over the two others with four shots. In the twinkling of an eye she deprived of life the bodies of these four tigers. Until now such shooting was never seen, that from the top of an elephant and the inside of a howdah six shots should be made and not one miss, so that the four

beasts found no opportunity to spring or move. As a reward for this good shooting I gave her a pair of bracelets of diamonds worth 100,000 rupees and scattered 1000 *ashrafis* [gold mohurs].

—59—

ELEPHANTS' BATHS.

[Jahangir's *Memoirs.*]

Among animals, elephants have the greatest liking for water, they delight to go into the water, notwithstanding the
1617. winter and the coldness of the air, and if there be no water into which they can go, they will take it from a water bag with their trunks and pour it over their bodies. It occurred to me that however much an elephant delights in water and it is suited to their temperament, yet in the winter the cold water must affect them. I accordingly ordered the water to be made milk-warm before they drew it into their trunks. On other days when they poured water over themselves they evidently shivered, but with warm water on the contrary they were delighted. This plan is entirely my own idea.

—60—

JAHANGIR FORESWEARS SHOOTING.

[Jahangir's *Memoirs.*]

Prince Shuja', the darling son of my son Shah-Jahan, who was being brought up in the chaste lap of Nur-Jahan Begam,
1618. and towards whom I have so much affection that he is dearer to me than life, was attacked by a specially infantile disease. As visible remedies were hopeless,

by way of humility and submission I rubbed the head of supplication on the Court of the gracious Ruler who cherishes his slaves, and begged for the child's recovery. In this state it occurred to me that,—as I had made a vow [seventeen years ago] to my God that after I had passed my fiftieth year this suppliant would give up hunting with bullet and gun, and would injure no creature with his own hand,—if for the sake of [the child's] safety I were to give up shooting from the present date, it was possible that his life would become the means of preserving the lives of many animals, and God Almighty might give him to me. In fine, with true purpose and sincere belief I vowed to God that thenceforward I would not harm any living thing with my own hand. By the grace of God his illness diminished.

—61—

SIR THOMAS ROE'S RECEPTION.

[Roe's *Embassy.*]

Jan. 10. I went to Court at 4 in the evening to the Durbar, which is the place where the Mogul sits out daily to entertain
1616. strangers, to receive petitions, to give commands, to see and to be seen. To digress a little from my reception and to declare the customs of the Court will enlighten the future discourse. The King hath no man but eunuchs that comes within the lodgings or retiring rooms of his house. His women watch within and guard him with manly weapons. They do justice one upon another for offences. He comes every morning to a window called the *Jharokha* looking into a plain before his gate, and shows himself to the common people. At noon he returns thither and sits some hours to

see the fight of elephants and wild beasts; under him within a rail attend the men of rank; from whence he retires to sleep among his women. At afternoon he returns to the Durbar before mentioned. At 8 after supper he comes down to the *Ghuzlkhana*, a fair court where in the midst is a throne erected of freestone wherein he sits, but sometimes below in a chair; to which are none admitted but of great quality, and few of those without leave; where he discourses of all matters with great affability. There is no business done with him concerning the state, government, disposition of war or peace, but at one of these two last places, where it is publicly propounded and resolved and so registered, which [register] if it were worth the curiosity might be seen for two shillings, but the common base people know as much as the council, and the news every day is the King's new resolutions tossed and censured by every rascal. This course is unchangeable, except sickness or drink prevent it; which must be known, for as all his subjects are slaves, so is he in a kind of reciprocal bondage, for he is tied to observe these hours and customs so precisely that if he were unseen one day, and no sufficient reason rendered, the people would mutiny; two days no reason can excuse, but that he must consent to open his doors and be seen by some to satisfy others. On Tuesday at the *Jharokha* he sits in judgement, never refusing the poorest man's complaint, where he hears with patience both parts; and sometimes sees with too much delight in blood the execution done by his elephants.

At the Durbar I was led right before him at the entrance of an outer rail, where met me two principal noble slaves to conduct me nearer. I had required before my going leave to use the customs of my country, which was freely granted, so that I would perform them punctually. When I entered within the first rail I made an obeisance; entering in the inward rail another; and when I came under the King a third. The place is a great court, whither resort all sorts of people. The King sits in a little gallery overhead; ambassadors, the great men, and strangers of quality within the inmost rail under him, raised from the ground, covered with canopies of velvet and silk, under foot laid with good carpets; the meaner men representing gentry within the first rail, the people without in a base court, but so that all may see the King. This sitting out hath so much affinity with a theatre,—the manner of the King in his gallery, the great men lifted on a stage as actors; the vulgar below gazing on — that an easy description will inform of the place and fashion.

The King prevented my dull interpreter, bidding me welcome as to the brother of my Master. I delivered his Majesty's letter translated; and after my commission, whereon he looked curiously; after my presents, which were well received. He asked some questions, and with a seeming care of my health, offering me his physicians, and advising me to keep my house until I had recovered strength; and if in the interim I needed anything I should freely send to him and obtain my desires. He dismissed me with more favour and outward grace (if by the Christians we were not flattered) than was ever shown to any ambassador, either of the Turk or Persian, or other whatsoever.

—62—

ROE PRESENTS A PICTURE.

[Roe's *Embassy.*]

July 13. [I said to Asaf Khan that] I had a picture of a friend of mine that I esteemed very much, and was for curiosity rare, which I would give his Majesty as a present, seeing he so much affected that art; assuring myself he never saw any equal to it, neither was anything more esteemed of me. Within half an hour two of the King's servants came for me, and Asaf Khan asked me for my little picture and presented it to the King. He took extreme content, showing it to every man near him; at last sent for his chief painter, demanding his opinion. The fool answered he could make as good. Whereat the King turned to me, saying, My man saith he can do the like and as well as this: what say you? I replied, I know the contrary. But if he doth, said he, what will you say? I answered, I would give 10,000 rupees for such a copy of his hand, for I know none in Europe but the same master can perform it. Nay, said the King, I will call four painters, my chief workmen, and what will you give me if they make one so like that you shall not know your own? . . . What wager would I lay? I replied, I knew not what to offer in wager to so great a prince, nor became it me to name it; but if his Majesty were pleased, I would lay any in my power to pay. Why, said he, if you will not lay with me, lay with the painter. I answered, No, Sir, as I am unfit with your Majesty, so your painter is no equal match to me; but I will wager with Asaf Khan or any of your lords. So he commanded Asaf Khan, who offered 5000 rupees. I replied I was content, but money was no honourable bet, especially among friends: but I would lay a good horse. So the match was agreed on; but Asaf Khan recanted in private.

1616.

After the King fell drinking of our Alicante, giving tastes to divers, and then sent for a full bottle, and drinking one cup sent it to me. So he turned to sleep; the candles were popped out, and I groped my way out of doors.

August 6. I was sent for to the Durbar. The business was about a Picture I had lately given the King and was confident no man in India could equal it. So soon as I came he asked me what would I give the painter that had made a copy so like it that I should not know mine own. I answered, a Painter's reward—50 rupees. The King replied that his Painter was a caballero, and that too small a gift; to which I answered, I gave my picture with a good heart, esteeming it rare, and meant not to make comparisons or wagers; if his servant had done as well, and would not accept of my gift, his Majesty was most fit to reward him. So with many passages of jests, mirth and brags concerning the arts of his country, he fell to ask me questions. How often I drank a day, and how much, and what? What in England? What beer was? How made? and whether I could make it here? in all which I satisfied his great demands of state. He concluded that I should come to the *Ghuzlkhana* and then I should see the pictures. At night he sent for me, being hasty to triumph in his workman, and showed me six pictures, 5 made by his man, all pasted on one table, so like that I was by candlelight troubled to discern which was which; I confess beyond all expectation; yet I showed mine own and the differences, which were in art apparent, but not to be judged by the common eye. But for that at first sight I knew it not, he was very merry and joyful and craked like a Northern man.

—63—

JAHANGIR AS ART-CRITIC.

[Jahangir's *Memoirs.*]

On this day Abu-l-Hasan the painter, who has been honoured with the title of Nadir-az-Zaman [phœnix of the age], drew

the picture of my accession as the frontispiece to the Jahangir-
1618. nama [my memoirs] and brought it to me. As it was worthy of all praise, he received endless honours. His work was perfect and his picture is one of the masterpieces of the age. At the present time he has no rival or equal. If at this time the masters 'Abd-al-Hayy and Bihzad were alive they would do him justice. Also Ustad Mansur [Nakkash] has become such a master in painting that he has the title of Nadir-el-Asr [wonder of the era], and in the art of drawing is unique in his generation. In my father's reign and mine these two men had no third.

As regards myself, my admiration of painting and practice in judging it have arrived at such a point that when any work is brought before me, either of deceased artists or of those of the present day, without the names being told me, I say on the spur of the moment that it is the work of such and such a man. And if there be a picture containing many portraits, and each face be the work of a different master, I can discover which face is the work of each of them. If any other person has put in the eye and eyebrow of a face, I can perceive whose work the original face is, and who has painted the eye and eyebrows.

— 64 —

A BIRTHDAY FEAST.

[Roe's *Embassy.*]

This day was the Birth of the King and solemnized as a great feast, wherein the King is weighed against some jewels,
2 Sept. 1616. gold, stuffs of gold and silver, silk, butter, rice, fruit, and many other things of every sort a little; which is given to the Brahmans. At night about ten of the clock he sent for me. I was abed. When

I came I found him sitting cross-legged on a little throne, all clad in diamonds, pearls and rubies; before him a table of gold: on it about 50 pieces of gold plate set all with stones, some very great and extremely rich, some of less value, but all of them almost covered with small stones; his nobility about him in their best equipage, whom he commanded to drink frolicly, several wines standing by in great flagons. When I came in he asked for the picture. I showed him two. He seemed astonished at one of them and confessed he never saw so much art, so much beauty, and conjured me to tell him truly whether ever such a woman lived. I assured him that there did one live that this did resemble in all things but perfection, and was now dead. . . . .

Then he sent me word that it was his birthday and that all men did make merry, and to ask if I would drink with them. I answered, Whatsoever his Majesty commanded: I wished him many prosperous days and that this ceremony might be renewed 100 years. He asked me what wine, whether of the grape or made, whether strong or small. I replied, What he commanded, hoping he would not command too much nor too strong. So he called for a cup of gold of mingled wine, half of the grape, half artificial, and drank, causing it to be filled, and sent it by one of his nobles to me with this message: that I should drink it twice, thrice, four or five times off for his sake, and accept of the cup and appurtenances as a present. I drank a little, but it was more strong than ever I tasted, so that it made me sneeze, whereat he laughed, and called for raisins, almonds and sliced lemons, which were brought me on a plate of gold and bade me eat and drink what I would, and no more. Thus he made frolic and sent me word he more esteemed me than ever any Frank and demanded if I were merry at eating the wild boar he sent me a few days before?

How I dressed it? and such compliments; that I should want nothing in his land. Then he threw about to those that stood below two chargers of new rupees and among us two chargers of hollow almonds of gold and silver mingled; but I would not scramble as did his great men; for I saw his son took up none. Then he gave *shashes* [turban cloths] of gold and girdles to all the musicians and waiters and to many others. So drinking and commanding others, his Majesty and all his lords became the finest men I ever saw, of a thousand fancies. But his son, Asaf Khan, and some two old men, and the late King of Kandahar, and myself forbare. When he could not hold up his head, he lay down to sleep, and we all departed.

October 25. Though drunkenness be a common and a glorious vice, and an exercise of the King's, yet it is so strictly forbidden that no man can enter the *Ghuzlkhana* where the King sits but the porters smell his breath, and if he have but tasted wine, is not suffered to come in: and if the reason is known of his absence, shall with difficulty escape the whip.

— 65 —

PRINCE KHURRAM'S ABSTINENCE.

[Jahangir's *Memoirs.*]

On Friday the weighing of my son Khurram took place. Up to the present year, when he is 24 years old, and is married and has children, he has never defiled himself
1616. with drinking wine. On this day, I said to him, "Baba, thou hast become the father of children, and kings and kings' sons have drunk wine. Today, which is the day of thy being weighed, I will give thee wine to drink, and give thee leave to drink it on feast days and at the time of the

New Year and at all great festivals. But thou must observe the path of moderation, for wise men do not consider it right to drink to such an extent as to destroy the understanding, and it is necessary that from drinking only profit should be derived." Avicenna, who is one of the most learned of physicians, has written this quatrain:

> Wine is a raging foe, a prudent friend;
> A little is an antidote, but much a snake's poison.
> In much there is no little injury;
> In a little there is much profit.

With much trouble wine was given to him.

—66—

THE CONSPIRACY AGAINST PRINCE KHUSRAU.

[Roe's *Embassy.*]

October 9. The ambitions of this young prince [Khurram] are open, the common talk of the people; yet his father suffers all, but intends him not the kingdom; for
1616. Sultan Khusrau, the eldest brother, is both extremely beloved and honoured of all men, almost adored, and very justly for his most noble parts; and this the King knows and loves: but thinks his liberty would diminish his own glory and sees not that this sly youth [Khurram] doth more darken him by ambitious practices than the other could by virtuous actions. Thus he nourisheth division and emulation between the brethren and putteth such power in the hand of the younger, supposing he can undo it at his pleasure, that the wisest foresee a rending and tearing of these kingdoms by division when the King shall pay the debt of nature, and that all parts will be torn and destroyed by a civil war.

The history of this country for the variety of subject and the many practices in the time of Akbar, father of this king, by him then prince, and these later troubles, were not unworthy committing to writing; but because they are of so remote parts many will despise them [and] because the people are esteemed barbarous few will believe them; therefore I content myself with the contemplation, but I could deliver as many rare and cunning passages of State, subtle evasions, policies, answers, and adages, as I believe for one age would not be easily equalled. Only one that passed lately I cannot omit, to show wisdom and patience in a father, faith in a servant, falsehood in a brother, impudent boldness in a faction that dare attempt anything when the highest Majesty gives them liberty beyond either the law of their own condition or the limits of patience and reason.

The prince Sultan Khurram, Nur-Mahall the dear queen, aunt to his wife, Asaf Khan his father-in-law, brother to the queen, and I'timad-ad-daula, father to them both, being that they now govern all and dare attempt anything, resolved it was not possible for them to stand if the prince Sultan Khusrau lived, whom the nobility loved, and whose delivery or life would punish their ambitions in time; therefore practised how to bring him into their power, that poison might end him. Nur-Mahall attempts the king with the false tears of woman's bewitching flattery: that Sultan Khusrau was not safe nor his aspiring thoughts deposed. The King hears, soothes it, but would not understand more than she delivered plainly. This failing, they took opportunity of the King's being drunk the prince, I'timad-ad-daula, and Asaf Khan moved the King that, for the safety of Sultan Khusrau and his honour, it were fitter he were in the keeping of his brother, whose companies would be pleasing one to the other and his safety more regarded than in the hands of a Rajput Gentile (to whom the King had committed him); therefore they humbly desired his Majesty that he might be delivered into the hands of his dear brother; which the King granted, and so fell asleep. [But Anup Rai, the Rajput Raja] refuseth to deliver up his charge [and] in the morning came to the King with the demand of the prince, his refusal and answer; and added that his Majesty had given him charge of his son and made him the commander of 4000 horse, with all which he would die at the gate rather than deliver the prince to his enemies. If his Majesty required him he was ready to do his will, but he would provide for his own innocency. The King replied: You have done honestly, faithfully: you have answered discreetly: continue your purpose and take no knowledge of any commands: I will not seem to know this, neither do you stir farther: hold your faith, and let us see how far they will prosecute it.

October 17. The King, who had yielded himself into the hands of a woman, could not defend his son from their practices. He either sees not the ambition or trusts it too far in confidence of his own power, and consents: so that this day he [Khusrau] was delivered up, the soldiers of Anup Rai discharged, and a supply of Asaf Khan's planted about him, with assistance of 200 of the prince's [Khurram's] horse. His sister and divers women in the seraglio mourn, refuse their meat, cry out of the king's dotage and cruelty, and profess that if he die then will 100 of his kindred burn with him in memory of the king's bloodiness to his worthiest son. The King gives fair words, protesteth no intent of ill towards the prince, and promiseth his delivery, and sends Nur-Mahall to appease these enraged ladies; but they curse, threaten, and refuse to see her. The common people all murmur. New hopes are spread of his delivery, and soon allayed; every man tells news according to his fears or desires.

But the poor prince remains in the tiger's power, refuseth meat, and requires his father to take his life and not to let it be the triumph and delight of his enemies. The whole Court is in a whisper; the nobility sad; the multitude, like itself, full of tumour and noise, without head or foot; only it rages but bends itself upon no direct road. The issue is very dangerous.

November 2. There is now a great whisper in Court about a new affinity of Sultan Khusrau and Asaf Khan, and great hope of his liberty. The wisdom and goodness of the King appears above the malice of others, and Nur-Mahall fulfils the observation that in all actions of consequence in a Court, especially in faction, a woman is not only always an ingredient, but commonly a principal drug and of most virtue; she shows that they are not incapable of conducting business, nor herself void of wit and subtlety.

February 3. Departing out of the road of the camp for ease and shade, and resting under a tree for the same commodities,
1617. came upon me Sultan Khusrau, the King's eldest restrained son, riding upon an elephant with no great guard nor attendance; who called for me and with some gentle and familiar questions, full of courtesy and affability, he departed. His person is good and countenance cheerful, his beard grown to his girdle. This only I noted, that his questions showed ignorance of all passages at Court, insomuch he never heard of any ambassador nor English.

August 24. The prince Sultan Khusrau had his first day of hoped liberty, and came to take air and pleasure at the banquetting house by me.

—67—

JAHANGIR'S TRAVELLING CAMP.

[Roe's *Embassy.*]

November 2. Returning I viewed the laskar [camp] which is one of the wonders of my little experience, that I had seen
1616. it finished and set up in 4 hours, the circuit being little less than 20 English miles, the length some ways 3 *kos*, comprehending the skirts; and [in] the middle, wherein the streets are orderly, and tents joined, are all sorts of shops and distinguished so by rule that every man knows readily where to seek his wants, every man of quality and every trade being limited how far from the King's tents he shall pitch, what ground he shall use, and on what side, without alteration; which as it lies together may equal almost any town in Europe for greatness. Only a musket shot every way no man approacheth the *toshakhana* royal, which is now kept so strict that none are admitted but by name, and the time of the Durbar in the evening is omitted and spent in hunting or hawking or on tanks by boats, in which the King takes wonderful delight, and his barques are removed on carts with him.

—68—

FLUTE-PLAYER AND STORY-TELLER WEIGHED.

[Jahangir's *Memoirs.*]

Ustad Muhammad, the flute-player (*Nayi*), who was unequalled in his craft, was sent by my son Khurram at my
1617. summons. I had heard some of his musical pieces, and he played a tune which he had composed for an ode in my name. I ordered him to be weighed against

rupees; this came to 6,300 rupees. I also gave him an elephant with a howdah, and I ordered him to ride in it and having packed his rupees about him to proceed to his lodging. Mulla Asad, the story-teller, one of the servants of Mirza Ghazi, came on the same day from Tatta and waited on me. As he was a reciter and story-teller full of sweetness and smartness, I liked his society, and I made him happy with this title of Mahzuz Khan and gave him 1,000 rupees, a dress of honour, a horse, an elephant, and a palanquin. After some days I ordered him to be weighed against rupees, and his weight came up to 4,400. He was raised to the *mansab* (command) of 200 personal and 20 horse. I ordered him always to be present at the meetings for talk.

On the same day they brought to my private fruit-house many mangoes from all parts of the Deccan, Burhanpur, Gujarat, and the parganas of Malwa. Although this province is well known and celebrated for the sweetness, freedom from stringiness, and size of its mangoes, and there are few to equal them, so that I often ordered them to be weighed in my presence, when they were shown to rise to a sir [2 lbs.] or a sir and a quarter—yet in sweetness of water and delicious flavour and digestibility the mangoes of Chapramau [in Sarkar Kanauj] in the province of Agra are superior to all the mangoes in India.

—69—

JAHANGIR AND A FAKIR.

[Roe's *Embassy.*]

December 18. I visited the king, who having been at his sports, and his quarry of fowl and fish lying before him, he desired me to take my choice, and so distributed the remainder to his nobility. I found him sitting on his throne, and a beggar at his feet, a poor silly old man, all ashed, ragged, and patched, with a young rogue attending him. With this kind of professed poor holy men the country abounds, and are held in great reverence; but for works of chastisement of their bodies and voluntary sufferings they exceed the brags of all heretics or idolaters. This miserable wretch, clothed in rags, crowned with feathers, covered with ashes, his Majesty talked with about an hour, with such familiarity and show of kindness that it must needs argue an humility not found easily among kings. The beggar sate, which his [the king's] son dare not do. He gave the King a present, a cake, ashed, burnt on the coals, made by himself of coarse grain, which the King accepted most willingly, and broke one bit and ate it, which a dainty mouth could scarce have done. After he took the clout and wrapt it up and put it in the poor man's bosom, and sent for 100 rupees and with his own hands poured them into the poor man's lap, and what fell beside gathered up for him. When his collation of banquetting and drink came, whatsoever he took to eat, he brake and gave the beggar half; and after many strange humiliations and charities, rising, the old wretch not being nimble, he took him up in his arms, which no cleanly body durst have touched, embracing him; and 3 times laying his hand on his heart, calling him father, he left him, and all us, and me, in admiration of such virtue in a heathen prince. Which I mention with envy and sorrow, that we having the true vine should bring forth crabs and a bastard stock grapes; that either our Christian princes had this devotion or that this zeal were guided by a true light of the Gospel.

1616.

— 70 —

GOSAÏN JADRUP.

[Jahangir's *Memoirs.*]

On Saturday for the second time my desire for the company of Jadrup increased. After performing the midday devotions,
1618. I embarked in a boat and hastened to meet him
and at the close of day I ran and enjoyed his society in the retirement of his cell. I heard many sublime words of religious duties and knowledge of divine things. Without exaggeration, he sets forth clearly the doctrines of wholesome Sufism and one can find delight in his society. He is sixty years of age. He was twenty-two when, forsaking all external attachments, he placed the foot of determination on the high-road of asceticism, and for thirty-eight years he had lived in the garment of nakedness.

My desire to see Gosaïn Jadrup again increased, and hastening to his hut I enjoyed his society. Sublime words were
1619. spoken between us. God Almighty has granted him
an unusual grace, a lofty understanding, an exalted nature, and keen intellectual powers, with a God-gifted knowledge and a heart free from the attachments of the world, so that, putting behind his back the world and all that is in it, he sips content in the corner of solitude and without wants. He has chosen of worldly goods half a yard [*gaz*] of old cotton, like a woman's veil, and a piece of earthenware to drink water from, and in winter and summer and the rainy season lives naked and with head and feet bare. He has made a hole in which he can turn round with a hundred difficulties and tortures, with a passage that a sucking child could hardly be

passed through. On Wednesday I again went and bade him good-bye. Undoubtedly parting from him weighed upon my mind, which desires the truth.

—71—

THE GOLDEN AGE OF SHAH JAHAN.

[Rai Bhara Mal: *Lubb-at-tawarikh.*]

The means employed by the King in these happy times to protect and nourish his people, his knowledge of what made
1628-59. for their welfare, his administration by honest and intelligent officers, the auditing of accounts, his care of the crown lands and their tenants, and encouragement of agriculture and the collection of revenue, together with his punishment and admonition of evil-doers, oppressors, and malcontents, all tended to the prosperity of the empire. The pargana which had brought in three lacs in Akbar's reign now yielded ten, though some fell short, and those who increased the revenue by careful agriculture were rewarded, and *vice versa.* The expenditure of former reigns was not a fourth of the cost of this reign, and yet the King quickly amassed a treasure which would have taken years to accumulate under his predecessors. Notwithstanding the extent of the country, plaints were so rare that only one day a week was assigned to the administration of justice, and seldom did even twenty plaintiffs appear on that day, to his Majesty's disappointment. But if offenders were discovered, the local authorities generally tried them on the spot, with right of appeal to the governor or Diwan or Kazi, when the cause was reviewed and judgement given with great care and discrimination, lest it should come to the King's ears that justice had not been done.

— 72 —

TAKING OF HUGLI PORT.

['Abd-al-Hamid Lahori : *Badshah-nama.*]

Under the rule of the Bengalis a party of Frank merchants, who are inhabitants of Sundip, came trading to Satganw.

1631. One *kos* above that place they occupied some ground on the bank of the estuary. Under the pretence that a building was necessary for their dealings they set up some houses in the Bengal style. Gradually, by the negligence of the rulers, these Europeans increased in number and erected solid buildings protected by guns and muskets, and in due course the considerable Port of Hugli grew up, frequented by European ships, and a trade was established. The markets of Satganw declined, but the villages and lands of Hugli were on both sides of the river and were obtained at a low rent. Some of the people by force, but more by hopes of gain, they infected with their Christian teaching and sent them in ships to Europe. They seized and carried off every-one they could lay hands on along the river banks.

The Emperor appointed Kasim Khan to the government of Bengal and laid on him the duty of suppressing these obnoxious people. Troops were to be sent by water and land so that the difficult task might be quickly accomplished. Kasim Khan made preparations and at the close of the cold season in Sha'ban 1040 (1631) he sent his son Inayat-Allah with others to conquer Hugli. They formed a bridge of boats between Hugli and the sea, so that ships could not get down ; thus the flight of the enemy was prevented.

The attack was made on 2nd Zu-l-Hijja by the boatmen on the river and by the troops on land. An inhabited place outside the ditch was taken and its occupiers slain; detachments scoured the surrounding villages and sent the Christians to hell; and for three months and a half the strong place was besieged. Sometimes the infidels fought, sometimes they made overtures of peace, delaying in hope of succour from their countrymen. With base treachery they pretended to make proposals of peace and sent nearly a lac of rupees as tribute, while at the same time they ordered 7000 musketeers who were in their service to open fire. At length the besiegers sent their pioneers to work upon the ditch just by the church, where it was not so broad or deep, and they dug channels and drew off the water. Mines were pushed on from the trenches, but two of these were discovered by the enemy and frustrated. The middle mine was carried under the highest and strongest of the buildings and charged, and the troops were massed before this part to draw the garrison to it. When a large number were mustered there, a heavy fusilade was opened and the mine was fired. The building was blown up and the many infidels collected around it were sent flying into the air. The warriors of Islam rushed to the assault. Some of the infidels found their way to hell by water, but some thousands gained the ships. One large ship, which had nearly 2000 men and women on board, they blew up, lest she should fall into the hands of the Muslims. Only two boats out of the hundreds in the river escaped. From the beginning to the end of the siege altogether nearly ten thousand of the enemy, men and women, old and young, were killed, drowned, burnt, or blown up, and 4400 of both sexes were made prisoners. Nearly 1000 brave warriors of the Imperial army won the crown of martyrdom.

[Bernier's *Travels*: Constable's edition.]

The miseries of these people is unparalleled in the history of modern times; it nearly resembled the grievous captivity of Babylon; for even the children, priests, and monks shared the universal doom. The handsome women, as well married as single, became inmates of the seraglio; those of a more advanced age or of inferior beauty were distributed among the Omrahs [Amirs]; little children underwent the rite of circumcision and were made pages; and the men of adult age, allured for the most part by fair promises or terrified by the daily threat of throwing them under the feet of elephants, renounced the Christian faith. Some of the monks, however, remained faithful to their creed and were conveyed to Goa and other Portuguese settlements by the kind exertions of the Jesuits and missionaries at Agra, who, notwithstanding all this calamity, continued in their dwelling and were enabled to accomplish their benevolent purpose by the powerful aid of money and the warm intercession of their friends. Before the catastrophe at Hugli, the missionaries had not escaped the resentment of Shah Jahan: he ordered the large and handsome church at Agra, which, together with one at Lahore, had been erected during the reign of Jahangir, to be demolished. A high steeple stood up on this church, with a bell the sound of which was heard in every part of the city.

— 73 —

THE RAJPUTS.

[Bernier's *Travels.*]

These people are educated from one generation to another in the profession of arms. Parcels of land are assigned to them for their maintenance by the Rajas whose subjects they are, on condition that they shall appear in the field on the summons of their chieftain. They might be said to form a species of Gentile nobility, if the land were inalienable and descended to their children. From an early age they are accustomed to the use of opium, and I have sometimes been astonished to see the large quantities they swallow. On the day of battle they never fail to double the dose, and this drug so animates, or rather inebriates, them that they rush into the thickest of the combat insensible of danger. If the Raja himself be a brave man, he need never entertain an apprehension of being deserted by his followers: they only require to be well led, for their minds are made up to die in his presence rather than abandon him to his enemies. It is an interesting sight to see them on the eve of a battle, with the fumes of opium in their heads, embrace and bid adieu to one another as if certain of death. Who then can wonder that the Great Mogul, though a Muhammadan and as such an enemy to the Gentiles [Hindus], always keeps in his service a large retinue of Rajas, treating them with the same consideration as his other Omrahs and appointing them to important commands in his armies?

— 74 —

PRINCE DARA.

[Bernier's *Travels.*]

Dara was not deficient in good qualities: he was courteous in conversation, quick at repartee, polite, and extremely liberal: but he entertained too exalted an opinion

1658. of himself; believed he could accomplish everything by the powers of his own mind, and imagined that there existed no man from whose counsel he could derive benefit. He spoke disdainfully of those who ventured to advise him, and thus deterred his sincerest friends from disclosing the secret machinations of his brothers. He was also very irascible; apt to menace; abusive and insulting even to the greatest Omrahs [Amirs]; but his anger was seldom more than momentary. Born a Muhammadan, he continued to join in the exercises of that religion; but although thus publicly professing his adherence to its faith, Dara was in private a Gentile with Gentiles, and a Christian with Christians. He had constantly about him some of the Pundits or Gentile doctors, on whom he bestowed large pensions. He had, moreover, for some time lent a willing ear to the suggestions of the Rev. Father Busée, a Jesuit, in the truth and propriety of which he began to acquiesce. There are persons, however, who say that Dara was in reality destitute of all religion, and that these appearances were assumed only from motives of curiosity and for the sake of amusement; whilst according to others he became by turns a Christian and a Gentile from political considerations; wishing to ingratiate himself with the Christians who were pretty numerous in his corps of artillery, and also hoping to gain the affection of the Rajas and Gentile Princes tributary to the empire.

—75—

AT THE BATTLE OF SAMUGARH.

[Bernier's *Travels.*]

The preparations being completed, the artillery of both armies opened their fire, the invariable mode of commencing an engagement; and the arrows were already thick

1658. in the air, when suddenly there fell a shower of rain so violent as to interrupt the work of slaughter for a while. The weather had no sooner cleared than the sound of cannon was again heard, and Dara was at this time seen seated on a beautiful elephant of Ceylon, issuing his orders for a general onset; and placing himself at the head of a numerous body of horse, he advanced boldly towards the enemy's cannon. He was received with firmness and soon surrounded by heaps of slain. And not only the body which he led to the attack, but those by which he was followed were thrown into disorder. Still did he retain an admirable calmness and evince his immovable decision not to recede. He was observed on his elephant looking about him with an undaunted air and marking the progress of the action. The troops were animated by his example and the fugitives resumed their ranks; the charge was repeated, but he could not come up with the enemy before another volley carried death and disaster among the assailants: many took to flight, but the greater part seemed to have imbibed Dara's spirit and followed their intrepid commander until the cannon were forced and the iron chains disengaged, the enemy's camp entered, and the camels and infantry put completely to the rout.

It was now that, the cavalry of both armies coming into contact, the battle raged with the greatest fierceness. Showers of arrows obscured the air, Dara himself emptying his quiver; these weapons, however, produce little effect, nine out of ten flying over the soldiers' heads or falling short. The arrows discharged, the sword was drawn, and the contending squadrons fought hand to hand, both sides appearing to increase in obstinacy in proportion as the sword performed its murderous work. During the whole of this tremendous conflict, Dara afforded undeniable proof of invincible courage, raising the voice of encouragement and command, and performing such feats of valour that he succeeded at length in over-throwing the enemy's cavalry and compelling it to fly.

Aurangzib, who was at no great distance, and mounted also on an elephant, endeavoured, but without success, to retrieve the disasters of the day. Here I cannot avoid commending his bravery and resolution. He saw that nearly the whole of the army under his immediate command was defeated and put to flight; he found that Dara, notwithstanding the extreme ruggedness of the ground which separated them, evidently intended to rush upon his remaining little band: yet did he not betray the slightest symptom of fear, or even an inclination to retreat; but, calling many of his principal officers by name, called aloud to them "Dil-i yarana" ("Courage, my old friends")—I am repeating the exact words—"Khoda hai!" ("There *is* a God"). "What hope can we find in flight? Know ye not where is our Deccan? Khoda hai! Khoda hai!" And then, to remove all doubt of his resolution, and to show that he thought of nothing less than a retreat, he commanded that chains should be fastened round the feet of his elephant. . . . .

Dara left his own elephant a few minutes too soon, and was hurled from the pinnacle of glory to be numbered among the most miserable of princes.

[Manucci: *Storia do Mogor.*
Trans. Irvine.]

I saw in this action, as in so many others where I was afterwards present, that the only soldiers who fought were those well to the front. Of those more to the rear, although holding their bared swords in their hands, the Moguls did nothing but shout "Boquox, boquox!" (*Ba-Kush! Ba-Kush!*), and the Indians "Mar, Mar," that is to say, "Kill! Kill!". If those in the front advanced, those behind followed the example, and if the former retired the others fled, a custom of Hindustan quite contrary to that of Europe; and if they begin to take to flight, by no method is it possible to stop them.

—76—

DARA IN FLIGHT.

[Bernier's *Travels.*]

I had now been three days with Dara, whom I met on the road by the strangest chance imaginable; and being destitute of any medical attendant, he compelled me to accompany him in the capacity of physician. It was at break of day that the Governor's message [refusing a refuge at Ahmadabad] was delivered, and the shrieks of the females drew tears from every eye. We were all overwhelmed with confusion and dismay, at a loss what plan to recommend and ignorant of the fate which perhaps awaited us from hour to hour. We observed Dara stepping out, more dead than alive, speaking now to one, then to another; stopping and consulting even the commonest soldier. He saw consternation depicted on every countenance, and felt assured that he should be left without a single follower; but what was to become of him? whither must he go? to delay his departure was to accelerate his ruin.

1659.

—77—

DARA'S END.

[Bernier's *Travels.*]

Dara was now seen seated on a miserable and worn out elephant covered with filth; he no longer wore the necklace of large pearls which distinguishes the princes of Hindustan, nor the rich turban and embroidered coat; he and his son were now habited in dirty cloth of the coarsest texture, and his sorry turban was wrapped round with a Kashmir shawl or scarf resembling that worn by the meanest of the people. Such was the appearance of Dara when led through the bazars and every quarter of the city. I could not divest myself of the idea that some dreadful execution was about to take place. . . . . The crowd assembled upon this disgraceful occasion was immense; and everywhere I observed the people weeping and lamenting the fate of Dara in the most touching language. I took my station in one of the most conspicuous parts of the city, in the midst of the largest bazar; I was mounted on a good horse and accompanied by two servants and two intimate friends. From every side I heard piercing and distressing shrieks, for the Indian people have a very tender heart; men, women and children wailing as if some mighty calamity had happened to themselves.

Aurangzib was immediately made acquainted with the impression which this spectacle produced upon the public mind. A second council was consequently convened and the question discussed whether it was more expedient to conduct Dara to Gwalior, agreeably to the original intention, or to put him to death without further delay. . . . The charge of this atrocious murder was entrusted to a slave of the name of Nazar, who had been educated by Shah Jahan, but experienced some ill-treatment from Dara. The Prince, apprehensive that poison would be administered to him, was employed with [his son] Sipihr Shukoh in boiling lentils, when Nazar and four other ruffians entered his apartment. "My dear son," he cried out, "these men are come to murder us!". He then seized a small kitchen knife, the only weapon in his possession. One of the murderers having secured Sipihr Shukoh, the rest fell upon Dara, threw him down and while three of the assassins held him, Nazar decapitated his wretched victim. The head was instantly carried to Aurangzib, who commanded that it should be placed in a dish and that water should be brought. The blood was then washed from the face, and when it could no longer be doubted that it was indeed the head of Dara, he shed tears and said " Ah wretched one! let this shocking sight no more offend my eyes; but take away the head and let it be buried in Humayun's tomb."

—78—

CHARACTER OF AURANGZIB.

[Bakhtawar Khan : *Mir'at-i-'alam.*]

Be it known to the readers of this work that this humble slave of the Almighty is going to describe in a correct manner the excellent character, the worthy habits and the refined morals of this most virtuous monarch, according as he has witnessed them with his own eyes.

The Emperor, a great worshipper of God by temperament, is noted for his rigid attachment to religion. In his great
1659-1707. piety he passes whole nights in the palace mosque and keeps the company of devout men. In privacy he never sits on a throne. Before his accession he gave in alms part of his food and clothing and still devotes to alms the income of some villages near Delhi and of some salt tracts assigned to his privy purse. He keeps fast throughout Ramazan and reads the holy Koran in the assembly of religious men with whom he sits for six or even nine hours

of the night. From his youth he abstained from forbidden food and practices, and from his great holiness does nothing that is not pure and lawful. Though at the beginning of his reign he used to hear the exquisite voices of ravishing singers and brilliant instrumental performances, and himself understands music well, yet now for several years past, in his great restraint and self-denial, he entirely abstains from this joyous entertainment. He never wears clothes prohibited by religion, nor uses vessels of silver or gold. No unseemly talk, no word of backbiting or falsehood, is permitted at his Court. He appears twice or thrice daily in his audience chamber, with a mild and pleasing countenance, to dispense justice to petitioners, who come in numbers without hindrance and obtain redress. If any of them talks too much or acts improperly, he is not displeased and never knits his brows. By hearing their very words and watching their gestures he says that he acquires a habit of forbearance and toleration. Under the dictates of anger and passion he never passes sentence of death.

Hindu writers have been entirely excluded from holding public offices, and all the infidels' places of worship and great temples have been destroyed. His Majesty personally teaches the Muhammadan Profession of Faith to unbelievers, and awards favours to his converts. All over the country pensions and lands have been granted to learned men and professors and stipends to scholars. He ordered the remission of transit dues on grain, cloth, tobacco, and other goods, the collection of which and the prevention of smuggling had led to oppression. Muslims were exempted from taxes, and many requisitions were abolished, such as the confiscation of the estates of deceased landowners.

He has learnt the Koran by heart and written out two copies of it in an elegant Naskhi hand, and presented them to the holy cities of Mecca and Medina. He is a very elegant writer in prose, but though proficient in versification he abstains from it, agreeably to the words of God, "Poets deal in falsehood." He does not like to hear verses unless they hold a moral. The excellence of character and the purity of morals of this holy monarch are beyond expression.

[Bernier's *Travels.*]

Aurangzib, the third brother, was devoid of that urbanity and engaging presence so much admired in Dara, but he possessed a sounder judgement, and was more skilful in selecting for confidants such persons as were best qualified to serve him with faithfulness and ability. He distributed his presents with a liberal but discriminating hand among those whose good will it was essential to preserve or cultivate. He was reserved, subtle, and a complete master of the art of dissimulation. When at his father's court he feigned a devotion which he never felt and affected contempt for worldly grandeur while clandestinely endeavouring to pave the way to future elevation. Even when nominated Viceroy of the Deccan, he caused it to be believed that his feelings would be better gratified if permitted to turn Fakir, that is to say a beggar, a Dervish, or one who has renounced the world; that the wish nearest his heart was to pass the rest of his days in prayer or in offices of piety, and that he shrank from the cares and responsibility of government. Still his life had been one of undeviating intrigue and contrivance, conducted, however, with such admirable skill that every person in the court, excepting only his brother Dara, seemed to form an erroneous estimate of his character. The high opinion expressed by Shah Jahan of his son Aurangzib provoked the envy of Dara, and he would sometimes say to his intimate friends that of all his brothers the only one who excited his suspicion and filled him with alarm was "that *namazi*," or as we should say "that bigot," that ever-prayerful one.

My readers have no doubt condemned the means by which the reigning Mogul attained the summit of power. These means were indeed unjust and cruel; but it is not perhaps fair to judge him by the rigid rules which we apply to the character of European princes. In our quarter of the globe the succession to the crown is settled in favour of the eldest by wise and fixed laws; but in Hindustan the right of governing is usually disputed by all the sons of the deceased monarch, each of whom is reduced to the cruel alternative of sacrificing his brothers that he himself may reign, or of suffering his own life to be forfeited for the security and stability of the dominion of another. Yet even those who may maintain that the circumstances of country, birth, and education afford no palliation of the conduct pursued by Aurangzib, must admit that this Prince is endowed with a versatile and rare genius, that he is a consummate statesman, and a great King.

— 79 —

AT AN IMPERIAL LEVEE.

[Bernier's *Travels.*]

The King appeared seated upon his throne, at the end of the great hall, in the most magnificent attire. His vest was
1669. of white and delicately flowered satin, with a silk and gold embroidery of the finest texture. The turban, of gold cloth, had an aigrette whose base was composed

of diamonds of an extraordinary size and value, besides an Oriental topaz which may be pronounced unparalleled, exhibiting a lustre like the sun. A necklace of immense pearls, suspended from his neck, reached to his stomach, in the same manner as many of the Gentiles wear their strings of beads. The throne was supported by six massy feet, said to be of solid gold, sprinkled over with rubies, emeralds, and diamonds. It was constructed by Shah Jahan for the purpose of displaying the immense quantity of precious stones accumulated successively to the treasury from the spoils of ancient Rajas and Patans and the annual presents to the Monarch which every Omrah is bound to make on certain festivals. The construction and workmanship of the throne are not worthy of the materials; but two peacocks, covered with jewels and pearls are well conceived and executed.

At the foot of the throne were assembled all the Omrahs in splendid apparel, upon a platform surrounded by a silver railing and covered by a spacious canopy of brocade with deep fringes of gold. The pillars of the hall were hung with brocades of a gold ground, and flowered silken canopies were raised over the whole expanse of the extensive apartment fastened with red silken cords from which were suspended large tassels of silk and gold. The floor was covered entirely with carpets of the richest silk, of immense length and breadth. A tent was pitched outside, larger than the hall, to which it was joined by the top. It spread over half the court, and was completely enclosed by a great balustrade covered with plates of silver. Its supporters were pillars overlaid with silver, three of which were as thick and as high as the mast of a barque, the others smaller. The outside of this magnificent tent was red, and the inside lined with elegant Masulipatam chintzes, figured expressly for that very purpose with flowers so natural and colours so vivid that the tent seemed to be encompassed with real parterres.

On the third day of the festival the King, and after him several Omrahs, were weighed with a great deal of ceremony in large scales, which, as well as the weights, are, they say, of solid gold. I recollect that all the courtiers expressed much joy when it was found that Aurangzib weighed two pounds more than the year preceding.

—80—

A FAIR IN THE SERAGLIO.

[Bernier's *Travels.*]

A whimsical kind of fair is sometimes held during these festivities in the Mahall or royal seraglio; it is conducted by the handsomest and most engaging of the wives of the Omrahs and chief *Mansabdars* [great stipendiaries]. The articles exhibited are beautiful brocades, rich embroideries of the newest fashion, turbans elegantly worked on cloth of gold fine muslins worn by women of quality, and other articles of high price. These bewitching females act the part of traders, while the purchasers are the King, the Begams or princesses, and other distinguished ladies of the seraglio. If any Omrah's wife happens to have a handsome daughter, she never fails to accompany her mother, that she may be seen by the King and become known to the Begams. The charm of the fair is the ludicrous manner in which the King makes his bargains, frequently disputing for the value of a penny. He pretends that the good lady cannot possibly be in earnest, that the article is much too dear, that it is not equal to that he can find elsewhere, and that positively he will give no more than such a price. The woman on the other hand endeavours to sell to the best advantage, and when the King perseveres in offering what she considers too little money, high words frequently ensue and she fearlessly tells him that he is a worthless trader, a person ignorant of the value of merchandize, that her articles are too good for him and that he had better go where he can suit himself better, and similar jocular expressions. The Begams betray if possible a still greater anxiety to be served cheaply; high words are heard on every side, and the loud and scurrilous quarrels of the sellers and buyers make a complete farce. But sooner or later they agree upon the price; the princesses as well as the King buy right and left, pay in ready money, and often slip out of their hands, as if by accident, a few gold instead of silver rupees, intended as a compliment to the fair merchant or her pretty daughter. The present is received in the same unconscious manner, and the whole ends amidst jests and good-humour.

—81—

SUPPORT OF THE ARTS.

[Bernier's *Travels.*]

The arts in the Indies would long ago have lost their beauty and delicacy if the Monarch and principal Omrahs did not keep in their pay a number of artists, who work in their houses, teach the children, and are stimulated to exertion by the hope of reward and the fear of the whip. The protection afforded by powerful patrons to rich merchants and tradesmen, who pay the workmen rather higher wages, tends also to preserve the arts. Workshops occupied by skilful artisans would be vainly sought for in Delhi, which has very little to boast of in that respect. This is not owing to any inability in the people to cultivate the arts, for there are ingenious men in every part of India. Numerous are the instances of handsome pieces of workmanship made by persons destitute of tools and who can scarcely be said to have received instruction from a master. Sometimes they imitate so perfectly articles of European manufacture that the difference between the original and copy can hardly be discovered. Among other things the Indians make excellent muskets and fowling pieces, and such beautiful gold ornaments that it may be doubted if the exquisite workmanship of those articles can be exceeded by any European goldsmith. I have often admired the beauty, softness, and delicacy of their paintings and miniatures, and was particularly struck with the exploits of Akbar painted on a shield by a celebrated artist who is said to have been seven years in completing the picture. The Indian painters are chiefly deficient in just proportions and in the expression of the face. Want of genius, therefore, is not the reason why works of superior art are not exhibited in the capital. The artists who arrive at any eminence are those only who are in the service of the king or of some powerful Omrah and who work exclusively for their patron.

— 82 —

SIVAJI.

[Khafi Khan: *Muntakhab-al-lubab.*]

The ancestors of the reprobate Sivaji derive from the line of the Ranas of Chitor, but his grandmother was of a Maratha tribe which claims to belong to an obscure branch of Rajputs.

1650-80. Sivaji became manager of the parganas of Poona and Supa for his father Sahu Bhoslah. He was remarkable for courage and quick wits, and in craft and guile he was a clever son of the devil, the father of fraud. In that country where all the hills rise to the sky and the jungles are dense with woods and bushes, he had an inaccessible lair. Like the zamindars of those parts he set about building forts in the hills. 'Adil Khan of Bijapur fell sick, and in the ensuing confusion Sivaji boldly and fraudulently seized the district with some of the neighbouring estates. This was the beginning of the system of tyranny which he and his descendants spread over the rest of the Konkan and all the Deccan. Whenever he heard of a prosperous town or a district inhabited by thriving farmers, he plundered and seized it. He gathered a large force of Maratha robbers and plunderers, and began reducing fortresses. Day by day he increased in strength, reduced all the forts, and ravaged the country far and wide. He built some forts, till he had altogether forty, all well supplied with provisions and arms. Boldly raising the standard of rebellion, he became the most noted rebel of the Deccan.

Sivaji always strove to maintain the honour of the people in his territories. He persisted indeed in rebellion, plundering caravans, and troubling mankind; but he entirely abstained from other disgraceful acts, and was careful to respect the honour of the women and children of Muhammadans when they fell into his hands. His orders about this were very strict, and to disobey them brought its punishment.

—83—

ATTACK ON THE MOGUL GENERAL.

[Khafi Khan.]

The Amir of Amirs Shayista Khan after taking several strong places went to Poona and lodged in a house built by
1663. that hell-dog Sivaji. Thence he sent out parties to destroy his power and take him prisoner. It was ordered that no one, especially a Maratha, armed or unarmed, should be admitted to the city or cantonment lines without a pass, except those in the imperial service, where no Maratha horseman was employed. Sivaji, beaten and dispirited, had retired into the rugged mountains and continually changed his retreat. One day a party of Maratha foot-soldiers went to the Kotwal of Poona and obtained a pass for 200 of their nation who were escorting a wedding party. A boy dressed up as a bridegroom escorted by a band of Marathas with drums and music entered the town early in the evening, and on the same day another party was admitted on the pretext that a number of the enemy had been caught and that this party were dragging them in by ropes, pinioned and bare-headed, abusing and reviling them as they went along. When they got to the place prearranged the whole number met and put on arms. At midnight they went to the cook-house of Shayista Khan's lodging, which was near the women's rooms. Between the two was a small window stopped up with mud and bricks. They went by a way well known to them and got into the kitchen. Some of the cooks were awake and busy, others were asleep. The intruders approached noiselessly, and as far as they could attacked and killed those who were awake and butchered the sleepers as they lay. So no

great alarm was raised. Then they set about opening the shut up windows into the house and the noise woke a servant on the other side of the wall. He went to Shayista Khan and reported what he had heard. The Amir scolded him and said it was one of the cooks who had got up to do their work. Some maidservants then appeared, one after the other, to say that a hole was being made through the wall. The Amir at this jumped up in great alarm and got hold of a bow and arrow and a spear. Just then some of the Marathas came up, and the Amir shot one, but the fellow got up to him and cut off his thumb. Two of the burglars fell into the tank, and another went down before the Amir's spear. In the hubbub two slave girls took Shayista Khan Amir al-Umara by the hand and dragged him to a place of safety. Other Marathas got into a guard-house and killed every man whom they found on his pillow, saying "This is how they keep watch." Some got into the band-room and in the Amir's name ordered the drums to be beaten; such a din was raised that none could hear another speak, and the noise made by the assailants waxed worse. They closed the doors. Abu-l-Fath, son of Shayista, a brave youth rushed forward and killed two or three, but was then killed himself. A man of consequence, who lived behind the house, hearing the uproar and finding the doors shut, tried to escape from a window by a rope ladder, but he was old and feeble, and rather like Shayista, and the Marathas mistook him for the Amir himself, and cut off his head. They attacked also two of the Amir's women, and served one so that when it came to burying her the remains had to be gathered in a basket. The other had thirty or forty wounds, but recovered. The housebreakers gave no thought to plundering, but made their way out of the house and went away.

—84—

SIVAJI'S ESCAPE FROM AGRA.

[Khafi Khan.]

After Sivaji returned angry and disappointed from the royal presence to his house [in Agra], orders were given to set
1666. guards round it. Reflecting on his former deeds and present state he was sadly troubled and thought of nothing else but delivering himself by some crafty device from his perilous situation. He feigned illness, took to his bed, and sent for the doctors. Then he announced his convalescence and sent presents to the physicians and attendants, food to Brahmans and grain and money to needy Muslims and Hindus, in large baskets covered with paper which he procured. Some of these were filled with sweetmeats and sent to amirs and fakirs. Swift horses were bought and were sent in charge of confederates, ostensibly as gifts to Brahmans, to a spot 14 leagues from the city. Á devoted comrade of his own figure took his place and wore his gold ring: he was to keep a muslim veil over his face and pretend to be asleep, but let the ring be visible. Then Sivaji and his son got into two of the big baskets and were carried out—as sweetmeats for the Brahmans and fakirs of Mathura! Arrived there on his horses, he shaved his beard and daubed his son's and his own face with ashes, crossed the Jumna, disguised as a fakir, at an unfrequented ferry, and journeyed by night to Benares, guided by swift Deccan runners whose business it is to disguise themselves and travel everywhere. It is said that they carried money and jewels enough for their needs in their walking canes. Sivaji continued his flight by way of Bihar, Patna and Chanda, where there are thick woods, he and his

followers frequently changing their disguises, and so going secretly reached Haidarabad where he told such stories and used such wiles that he wheedled and satisfied its king.

—85—

THE HINDU TAX (JIZYA).

[Khafi Khan.]

With the object of curbing the infidels and of distinguishing the land of the faithful from an infidel land, the *jizya* or
1680. poll-tax was imposed upon the Hindus throughout all the provinces. When this order was promulgated the Hindus round Delhi assembled in multitudes under the *jharokha* of the Emperor on the river front of the palace, declaring that they were unable to pay and praying for the revocation of the edict. But the Emperor would not listen to their complaints. One Sabbath as he went to prayers at the great mosque a vast crowd of Hindus thronged the road from palace to mosque. Moneychangers, shopkeepers, artisans, and workmen left off work and pushed into the press, and in spite of orders to clear the way the Emperor was unable to reach the mosque. Every moment the crowd swelled, and his equipage was brought to a standstill. Then the elephants were brought out and charged the mob, and many people were trodden to death. For days the Hindus went on assembling and complaining, but in the end they had to pay the jizya.

—86—

A PLEA FOR TOLERATION.

[Fryer's *New Account of East India*, etc.]

And now being returned he [Aurangzib] hardly forbears uttering his mind about his intention to make all the heathen

Musulmans, and told his chief Scrivener seriously one day
1680. that he must lose his place unless he would be of his religion. To which the subtle heathen replied, "Sahib,

"Sir, why will you do more than the Creator ever meant? You see hardly two faces bear exactly the same features. Look further into the world and behold the variety of creatures. God has made elephants, tigers, horses, camels, sheep, and oxen, of different figures, and man of a more exalted composure than the rest; whereas, had the Allwise Disposer of things thought it convenient, he might have rested contented in only one form; but any one of these in their several species glorifies their Maker. And so it has pleased God to permit variety of religions by which men worship and call upon him; nor can they go on in any one against his will, to which whatever is contrary cannot continue; and till he makes men to be of one mind, in vain does any go about to compel what he has ingrafted in their hearts."

This rational discourse kept the Brahman in his office, but could not quite extinguish his [master's] conceived prejudices against their superstitions.

—87—

THE HEROISM OF 'ABD-AR-RAZZAK LARI.

[Khafi Khan.]

In the last watch of the night Ruh-Allah Khan [by treachery within] entered the fortress of Golconda by ladders.
1687. Prince Muhammad A'zam, mounted on an elephant, had a large force ready to enter by the gate. Those who had got inside went to the gate and opened it, shouting victory.

Abd-ar-Razzak Lari heard this, and springing on a horse without a saddle, sword in one hand and shield in the other, followed by ten or a dozen men, he galloped to the open gate through which the Imperial troops were pouring in. His followers were scattered, but he alone, like a drop of water falling into the sea or a speck of dust quivering in a sunbeam, threw himself upon the advancing foe and fought with incredible fury and desperation, shouting that he was for Abu-l-Hasan to the death. Every step he took, thousands of swords made for him, and so often was he wounded that he was covered with gashes from the crown of his head to the nails of his feet. But his time was not yet come, and he fought his way down, still mounted, to the gate of the citadel. Twelve face wounds he received, and the skin of his forehead hung down over his eyes and nose. One eye was injured and his body cuts seemed as many as the stars. His horse too was covered with slashes and reared under his weight; he threw the reins on its neck, and with effort kept his seat. The horse bore him to a garden near the citadel, to the foot of an old cocoa-nut tree, by means of which he threw himself off. On the morning of the second day a party of men passing by recognized him and carried him on a mattress to a house, where his own men came and dressed his wounds.

The shouts and cries and groans and lamentations told Abu-l-Hasan that all was over for Golkonda. He went into his harim to comfort his women, ask their forgiveness, and take leave of them. Then, though his heart was sad, he controlled himself and went to his audience chamber and seated himself upon the *masnad* and waited for his unbidden guests. When dinner time came he ordered it to be served. As Ruh-Allah and the others entered, he saluted them all in turn and never for an instant abated his dignity. With complete calmness he received them courteously and conversed with them with graceful affability. He called for his horse and accompanied the amirs, carrying a great wealth of pearls upon his neck. When presented to Prince A'zam, he took off his necklace and gracefully offered it to the Prince, who put his hand on his back and did what he could to console and encourage him, and then conducted him to Aurangzib, who also received him very courteously and sent him later to the fortress of Daulatabad with a suitable allowance.

Meanwhile 'Abd-ar-Razzak, unconscious but with a spark of life left, was carried to Ruh-Allah's house. As soon as Safshikan Khan set eyes on him he cried out, " This is that rascally Lari! cut off his head and stick it on the gate. Ruh-Allah said it was scarcely human to decapitate a dying man without express orders. The case got to the ears of Aurangzib, who had heard of 'Abd-ar-Razzak's courage and loyalty, and he sent two surgeons, a European and a Hindu, to attend the wounded man and to report his condition daily to the Emperor. He sent also for Ruh-Allah and said that if Abu-l-Hasan had had one more servant like 'Abd-ar-Razzak, Golkonda would have held out much longer.

The surgeons reported that they had counted seventy wounds, besides wounds upon wounds uncountable. At the end of sixteen days he opened one eye and spoke a few stammering words, and in the end he got quite well.

—88—

THE ENGLISH AT BOMBAY.

[Khafi Khan.]

During the troubles [following the capture of an Imperial Mogul ship by an English vessel, under provocation,] I, the writer of this book, had the misfortune of seeing the English of Bombay when I was acting as agent for 'Abd-ar-

1694. Razzak Khan at the port of Surat. I had purchased goods to the value of nearly two lacs of rupees and had to convey them from Surat to 'Abd-ar-Razzak, then faujdar of Rahiri. My route was along the seashore through the lands of the Portuguese and English. 'Abd-ar-Razzak had been friendly with an Englishman formerly at Haidarabad, and this man kindly invited me to visit him at Bombay. I put my trust in God and went to the Englishman.

When I entered the fortress I noticed that there was on each side of the road a line of youths, twelve or fourteen years old, well dressed and shouldering capital muskets. Every step I advanced, young men with sprouting beards, handsome and well clothed, holding fine muskets, appeared on all sides. As I went on, I found Englishmen with long beards, of equal age and similar accoutrements and uniforms. Then I saw musketeers, young men, well dressed and mustered, drawn up in ranks. Further on were Englishmen in brocade, with white beards, and with muskets, drawn up in two ranks in perfect array. Next I saw English children, pretty and decked with pearls on the rims of their hats. And as far as the door of the house of the Englishman on both sides I found nearly 7,000 musketeers drawn up, dressed and accoutred as for a review. I then went straight up to where he was seated on a chair. He wished me Good-day, his usual form of salutation ; then he rose from his chair, embraced me, and signed to me to sit down on a chair opposite him. After a few kind enquiries, our conversation turned upon different things, pleasant and the reverse, bitter and sweet ; but all he said was in a kind and friendly spirit towards 'Abd-ar-Razzak. . . . When the interview was over, he proffered me entertainment after their fashion, but I accepted only *atr* and *pan* and was glad to escape.

— 89 —

AURANGZIB IN CAMP AT GALGALA.

[Gemelli Careri: *Voyage.*]

Saturday the 19th [March] I went to Gulalbar [so they call the king's quarters] and found the king was then giving audience, but there was such a multitude and confusion
1695. that I could not have a good sight of him. The king's and princes' tents took up three miles in compass, and were defended every way with palisadoes, ditches, and five hundred falconets. There were three gates into them, one for the harim or women, and two for the king and his court.

I was told the forces in this camp amounted to 60,000 horse and 1,000,000 of foot, for whose baggage there were 50,000 camels and 3,000 elephants; but that the sellers, merchants, and artificers were much more numerous, the whole camp being a moving city containing 5,000,000 of souls, and abounding not only in provisions but in all things that could be desired. There were 250 bazars or markets, every Omrah or general having one to serve his men. In short the camp was thirty miles about.

Monday the 21st, by the means of a Christian of Agra and an eunuch his friend, I had the fortune to be admitted to a private audience of the king. . . . I passed on into the second court and then into the royal tents and king's apartments, adorned with silks and cloth of gold. Finding the king in one of these rooms, sitting after the country manner, on rich carpets and pillows embroidered with gold; having made my obeisance after the Mogul fashion, I drew near, the same

Christian being my interpreter. He asked me of what kingdom of Europe I was, how long I had been come thence, where I had been, what I had come to his camp for, whether I would serve him, and whither I designed to go? . . . . He then asked me concerning the war between the Turk and European princes in Hungary; and having answered to the best of my knowledge, he dismissed me, the time of the public audience drawing near. I returned into the second court, enclosed with painted calicoes, ten spans high all about. . . .

Soon after the king came leaning on a staff forked at the top, several Omrahs and abundance of courtiers going before him. He had on a white vest tied under the right arm, according to the fashion of the Muhammadans to distinguish them from the Gentiles [Hindus], who tie it under the left. The cira or turban, of the same white stuff, was tied with a gold web, on which an emerald of a vast bigness appeared amidst four little ones. His shoes were after the Moorish fashion, and his legs naked without hose. Two servants put away the flies with long horsetails; another at the same time keeping off the sun with a green umbrella.

He was of a low stature, with a large nose, slender, and stooping with age. The whiteness of his round beard was more visible on his olive-coloured skin. When he was seated they gave him his scimitar and buckler, which he laid down on his left side within the throne. Then he made a sign with his left hand for those that had business to draw near; who being come up, two secretaries standing took their petitions, which they delivered to the king, telling him the contents. I admired to see him endorse them with his own hand, without spectacles, and by his cheerful smiling countenance seem to be pleased with the employment.

In the meanwhile the elephants were reviewed, that the king might see what condition they were in. When the Cornaccia (that is he who rides them) had uncovered the elephant's crupper for the king to view it, he made him turn his head towards the throne, and striking him on it three times, made him do his submission as often, by lifting up and lowering down his trunk. Then came Shah 'Alam's son and grandson, who having twice made their obeisance to the king, each time putting their hand to the ground, on their head, and on their breast, sat down on the first floor of the throne on the left. Then A'zam Shah, the king's second son, coming in and making the same submissions, he sate down on the second step. These princes wore silk vests with flowers of several colours, ciras adorned with precious stones, gold collars, jewels, rich sashes, scimitars, and bucklers hanging by their sides. Those that were not of the blood royal made three obeisances. . . .

When the audience was over, the king withdrew in the same order he came out; so did the princes, some getting into palanquins and others mounting stately horses covered with gold and precious stones. The Omrahs, who had stood all the while, returned also to their tents, followed by many elephants, some with seats on them, and some with colours flying, and attended by two troops of horse and two companies of foot. The Kotwal, who is like a provost-marshal against thieves, rode with a great trumpet of green copper, eight spans long, carried before him by a Moor on foot. That foolish trumpet made me laugh, because it made a noise much like that our swineherds make to call together their swine at night.

—90—

AURANGZIB'S POLICY.

[Fryer: *New Account of India.*]

He governs by this maxim: to create as many Omrahs or nobles out of the Moguls or Persian followers as may be fairly
1698. entrusted, but always with this policy—To remove them to remote charges from that where their *jagir* or annuity arises; as not thinking fit to trust them with forces or money in their allotted principalities, lest they should be tempted to unyoke themselves and slip their neck from the servitude imposed upon them; for which purpose their wives and children are left as pledges at Court while they follow the wars or are administering in cities and provinces; from whence, when they return, they have nothing they can call their own, only what they have cheated by false musters and a hard hand over both soldiers and people; which many times, too, when manifest, they are forced to refund to the king, though not restore to the oppressed; for all money, as well as goods and lands, are properly his, if he call for them.

—91—

THE EMPEROR'S OLD AGE.

[Manucci: *Storia di Mogor.*
Trans. W. Irvine.]

The old king still shows his eagerness for war by the gestures he uses on the march. When seated in his palanquin, he
1704. unsheathes his sword, makes cuts in the air, first one way, then another, and, smiling all the while, polishes it with a cloth, then returns it to its scabbard. He

does the same with his bow, to show that he can still let fly an arrow. But most of the time he sits doubled up, his head drooping. When his officers submit any petition or make report to him of any occurrence, he raises his head and straightens his back. He gives them such an answer as leaves no opening for reply, and still looks after his army in the minutest particulars. But those who are at a distance pay very little attention to his orders. They make excuses, they raise difficulties; and under cover of these pretexts, and by giving large sums to the officials at Court, they do just as they like. If he would only abandon his mock sainthood and behead a few of those in his empire, there would not be so much disorder, and he would be better obeyed.

— 92 —

LETTERS OF AURANGZIB.

[Iradat Khan.
Trans. Scott.]

To his son A'zam.

Health to thee! My heart is near thee. Old age is arrived; weakness subdues me, and strength has forsaken all my mem-
1707. bers. I came a stranger into this world, and a stranger I depart. I know nothing of myself, what I am or for what I am destined. The instant which has passed in power hath left only sorrow behind it. I have not been the guardian and protector of the empire. My valuable time has been passed vainly. I had a patron [conscience] in my own dwelling, but his glorious light was unseen by my dim sight. Life is not lasting; there is no vestige of departed breath, and all hopes from futurity are lost. The fever has left me, but nothing remains of me but skin and bone. . . . .

To his son Kam-Bakhsh.

My son, nearest to my heart! Though in the height of my power, and by God's permission, I gave you advice and took with you the greatest pains, yet, as it was not the Divine will, you did not attend with the ear of compliance. Now I depart a stranger and lament my own insignificance, what does it profit me? I carry with me the fruits of my sins and imperfections. Surprising Providence! I came here alone, and alone I depart. The leader of this caravan has deserted me. The fever, which troubled me for twelve days, has left me. Wherever I look I see nothing but the Divinity. My fears for the camp and followers are great; but alas! I know not myself. My back is bent with weakness and my feet have lost the power of motion. The breath which rose has gone and has left not even hope behind it. I have committed numerous crimes and know not with what punishments I may be seized. Though the Protector of mankind will guard the camp, yet care is incumbent also on the faithful, and on my sons. When I was alive no care was taken; and now I am gone, the consequences may be guessed. The guardianship of a people is the trust by God committed to my sons. Be cautious that none of the faithful are slain or that their miseries fall upon my head. I resign you, your mother and son, to God, as I myself am going. The agonies of death come on me fast. Bahadur Shah is still where he was, and his son is arrived near Hindustan. Bidar-Bakht is in Gujarat. Hayat-an-Nisa, who has beheld no afflictions of time till now, is full of sorrows. Regard the Begam as without concern. Udaipuri, your mother, was a partner in my illness and wishes to accompany me in death; but everything has its appointed time.

The domestics and courtiers, however deceitful, yet must not be ill-treated. It is necessary to gain your views by gentleness and art. Extend your feet no further than your skirt. The complaints of the unpaid troops are as before. Dara Shukoh, though of much judgment and good understanding, settled large pensions on his people, but paid them ill, and they were ever discontented. I am going. Whatever good or evil I have done, it was for you. Take it not amiss nor remember what offences I have done unto yourself, that account may not be demanded of me hereafter. No one has seen the departure of his own soul, but I see that mine is departing.

— 93 —

DEATH OF AURANGZIB.

[Musta'idd Khan: *Ma'asir-i-'Alamgiri.*]

The army encamped at Ahmadnagar on the 16th Shawwal in the 50th year of the reign. A year after this the King
1707. fell ill, but soon recovered his health and resumed the control of affairs. He appointed Shah Alam [Bahadur] governor of Malwa and Prince Kam-Bakhsh was sent to Bijapur. Only a few days after their departure he was seized with a burning fever, but he did not relax his devotions and every ordinance of religion was strictly observed. On Thursday evening he read a petition from a Khan who wished to devote 4,000 rupees, the price of an elephant, to be distributed by the Kazi as a propitiatory sacrifice. The King assented, and, though weak and suffering, wrote with his own hand on the petition that it was his earnest wish that this sacrifice should lead to his speedy dissolution. On the following morning, Friday, 28th Zu-l-Ka'ada

1118 [21 Feb. 1707] he performed the canonical prayers, and after finishing them returned to his sleeping room, where he remained absorbed in meditation. Faintness came on, still the fingers of the dying King continued mechanically to tell the beads of the rosary, and a quarter of the day later he breathed his last.

—94—

THE SIKHS.

[Khafi Khan.]

The violence of the Sikhs passed all bounds. The injuries and indignities they inflicted on Muslims and the destruction of mosques and tombs were to them righteous merito-

1714. rious acts. They had built a fort at Gurdaspur in the Panjab, ten or twelve days journey from Delhi, which would hold 50,000 or 60,000 horse and foot. They strengthened its towers and walls and occupied the cultivated fields around and ravaged the country from Lahore to Sirhind. 'Abd-as-Samad was sent as governor to Lahore with a picked army and guns. He engaged the vast forces of the Guru near his fort. The infidels fought so fiercely that the army of Islam was nearly overpowered; they showed repeatedly the greatest daring; great numbers were killed on both sides, but Mogul valour at length prevailed and the enemy were defeated and driven to their stronghold. Thence they made sallies by night with the utmost boldness and 'Abd-as-Samad Diler Jang had to throw up his entrenchment to protect his force in front of the fort. He raised batteries and pushed forward his approaches. In course of time the royal army succeeded in cutting off the enemy's supplies and the stores in the fort became exhausted. Reduced to extremity and despairing of life, the Sikhs offered to surrender on condition of their lives being spared. Diler Jang refused at first to give quarter, but finally he recommended them to beg the Emperor to pardon their crimes. Their chief Guru [Banda] with his child and his diwan [chancellor] and three or four thousand others became prisoners and received the predestined recompense of their deeds. Diler Jang put three or four thousand to the sword and filled the broad plain with blood like a dish. He sent two thousand heads stuffed with hay and a thousand captives in chains to the Emperor. Arrived at Delhi, orders were given that their faces should be blacked and wooden caps be put on the prisoners' heads, and that they should be set on camels, and the decapitated heads on spears, and thus brought into the city, escorted by the Bakhshi [paymaster] on his elephant, as a warning to all beholders. After they had passed before the Emperor, the Guru, his son, and a few companions were ordered to be confined in the fort; of the rest, two or three hundred of the miserable wretches were put to death every day before the kotwal's office and in the streets of the bazar. After all the Guru's followers had been killed, an order was given that his son should be slain in his presence, or rather that the boy, seven or eight years old, should be killed by his [father's] own hands to avenge the cruelty he had shown in slaying the sons of others. Afterwards the Guru himself was killed.

One youth's mother arrived with a reprieve [from the Emperor, Farrukh Siyar,] on the ground of alleged innocence, just as the executioner was standing with his bloody sword uplifted over the young man's head. She showed the order for his release. But the youth burst into reproaches, saying,

"My mother tells a falsehood. I join with heart and soul my fellow-believers in devotion to the Guru. Send me quickly after my companions."

—95—

THE BARHA BROTHERS.

[Jahangir's *Memoirs.*]

As in the Doab there are twelve [*bara*] villages near each other which are the country of these Sayyids, they have become known as the Sayyids of Barha. Some
1623. people may criticize their lineage, but their bravery is a convincing proof of their being Sayyids, for there has never been a battle in this reign in which they have not been conspicuous and in which some have not been killed.

[Khafi Khan.]

What has been said about them, and especially about Sayyid 'Abdallah [who died 1134 H.], in the matter of the death of Farrukh Siyar, the acceptance of bribes,
1722. the harsh dealing with farmers, and other bad courses which became grounds of public complaint,—these were all attributable to the evil influence of Ratan Chand, his diwan, who, being raised above his capacity, strove to vex the people. He was also pestered by fortune-seekers and needy adventurers whose claims he could not satisfy. Husain 'Ali Khan, before he was appointed to the Deccan, was exceeding averse to the extortion of money, but while he was there Muhkam Singh and other officials perverted his nature.

But both brothers were distinguished in their day for their generosity and leniency towards all men. The dwellers in those parts which were innocent of contumacy and selfishness made no complaints of the rule of the Sayyids. In liberality and benevolence to learned men and to the poor and in the patronage of men of merit Husain Ali excelled his elder brother and was the Hatim suited to his day. Numbers owed their comfort to the cooked food and raw grain he gave away. In the time of the scarcity at Aurangabad, he appropriated a large sum of money and a great quantity of grain to supply the needs of the poor and of widows. He was the originator of that large reservoir there, which in summer, when water is scarce, relieves the sufferings of the inhabitants. In their native country of Barha they built sarais, bridges, and other buildings for the public benefit. Sayyid 'Abdullah was notable for his patience, endurance, and wide sympathy.

—96—

NADIR SHAH AT DELHI.

[Anand Ram Mukhlis: *Tazkira.*]

Strange are the freaks of fortune: here was an army of 100,000 bold and well-armed horsemen held as it were in cap-
1739. tivity and all the resources of the Mogul Emperor and his nobles at the disposal of the Persian Red Caps! The Mogul monarchy seemed to all to be over.

When Nadir Shah's camp equipage arrived from Shahabad, the two Emperors set out for Delhi. They made the journey together on a lofty car. Muhammad Shah entered the citadel of Shahjahanabad in great pomp on the 8th Zu-l-Hijja, seated in the car; the conqueror followed on a horse the next day. By a strange cast of the dice, two monarchs who, but a short while before, found an empire too small to hold them both, were now dwellers within the same four walls.

The next day Nadir Shah returned the Indian ruler's visit and accepted the latter's offered presents. After the Shah's departure towards evening, a false rumour was spread through the city that he had been seriously wounded by a musket shot, and thus were sown the seeds of murder and rapine. The blackguards of the town collected in numbers and began indiscriminate plundering and destruction. Shots were fired throughout the night and in the darkness, where none could distinguish friend from foe, many of the Red Caps were killed in the narrow lanes, till there was hardly a spot not stained with their blood.

The result was that on the morning of the 11th the Persian Shah ordered the general slaughter of the inhabitants. The Chandni Chauk, the fruit market, the Daribah bazar, and the buildings round the great mosque, were set on fire and reduced to ashes. The inhabitants, one and all, were massacred. Here and there some opposition was offered, but in most places people were butchered unresistingly. The Persians laid violent hands upon everything and everybody; cloth, jewels, dishes of gold and silver, were acceptable spoil.

The writer beheld these horrors from his mansion situated in the Wakilpura Muhalla outside the city ; but, the Lord be praised, the work of destruction did not spread beyond the parts already named. Since the day when Timur captured Delhi and massacred its inhabitants up to the present year of the Hijra 1151, for 348 years the capital had been free from such visitations. The ruin of its beautiful streets and buildings was such that only the labour of years could restore Delhi to its former grandeur.

The massacre lasted half the day. Then the Persian Shah sent the Kotwal with a Persian guard through the streets to proclaim the stopping of slaughter. By degrees the violence of the flames subsided, but the bloodshed, devastation and ruin were irreparable. For a long time the streets were strewn with corpses like a garden with dead leaves. The city was reduced to ashes and looked like a burnt plain. All the royal jewels and property and the contents of the treasury were seized by the Persian conqueror, who thus acquired treasure to the sum of sixty lacs of rupees, and several thousand ashrafis; plate of gold worth a kror of rupees, and jewels, many of which were unique in beauty, valued at about fifty krors. The Peacock Throne alone had cost a kror. Elephants, horses, precious stuffs, whatever pleased the conqueror's eye, more than can be numbered, became his spoil. Writers were appointed to levy ransom from the inhabitants, watered by their tears. Not only was their money taken, but whole families were ruined. Many swallowed poison or stabbed themselves to death.

—97—

BATTLE OF PANIPAT.

[Muhammad Ja'far Shamlu: *Ta'rikh.*]

We turned back and reported the news to Ahmad Sultan that the Maratha army was steadily advancing to give battle.

He then made his dispositions and marshalled his ranks.

1761. Ahmad Sultan took his place in the centre and planted 2,000 camel swivels well in advance of his position. In their rear came 20,000 infantry *jazailchis*, backed by the royal servants. Behind these was the band, and Ahmad Sultan in the rear of this, supported by the 10,000 sabres of Red Cap cavalry and a force of Durranis, Ghilzais, etc. There were reserves on the right at half a league's distance, and also at the left, to give support in emergency. Both sides confronted each other till noon: then the gallant youths began the battle and dealt lusty blows, whilst the expert gunners of European race kindled the flames of war by firing their thunderous ordnance, and the rocket men of magical skill darted their hawklike missiles. As for musket bullets, the heroes recked them not, and in that scene of carnage their only dread was of cannon balls and rockets.

The battle raged till but three watches of the day remained. Bhao and Wiswas Rai, early in the combat, made such incessant charges that Ahmad Sultan, fearing he could not withstand them, sent an aide to make the ladies of his household mount swift horses and wait at his pavilion ready for instant flight. But the repeated charges of Mahmud Khan Gurd Bulbas at the head of eight or nine thousand dauntless and bloodthirsty Red Cap cavalry checked the Marathas. A ball struck Wiswas on the forehead and another Bhao on the side, and both betook themselves to the nethermost pits of hell. As soon as the Maratha army saw its chieftains fallen, it pursued the path of flight.

[*Ta'rikh-i-Ibrahim Khan.*]

The triumphant conquerors began eagerly to pillage the Maratha camp and managed to get possession of a boundless quantity of silver and jewels, 500 giant elephants, 50,000 horses, 1,000 camels, and two lacs of bullocks, with a vast amount of goods and camp equipage. Nearly 30,000 labourers, too, from the Deccan were made captives. Towards evening the 'Abdali Shah [Ahmad] went out to look at the slain and found great heaps of corpses and running streams of gore. Thirty-two mounds of slain were counted, and the ditch, protected by artillery, of such length that it would hold several lacs of men, besides cattle and baggage, was completely filled with the dead.

INDEX.

(Cross-references in brackets, authors and books in italics.)